MW00849455

WE NEED MORE PARTIES

SUPPORTED BY A GRANT FROM DEMOCRACY FUND

Publisher & Coeditor-in-Chief Deborah Chasman

Coeditor-in-Chief Joshua Cohen

Executive Editor Matt Lord

Assistant Editor Cameron Avery

Associate Publisher Jasmine Parmley

Circulation Manager Irina Costache

Contributing Editors Adom Getachew, Lily Hu, Walter Johnson, Robin D. G. Kelley, Paul Pierson, Becca Rothfeld, & Simon Torracinta

Production Assistant Ione Barrows

Editorial Fellow Finley Williams

Finance Manager Anthony DeMusis III

Board of Advisors Derek Schrier (Chair), Margo Beth Fleming, Archon Fung, Deborah Fung, Larry Kramer, Richard M. Locke, Jeff Mayersohn, Scott Nielsen, Robert Pollin, Hiram Samel, Kim Malone Scott, Brandon M. Terry, & Michael Voss

Interior Graphic Design Zak Jensen & Alex Camlin

Cover Design Alex Camlin

We Need More Parties is *Boston Review* issue 2024.3 (Forum 31 / 49.3 under former designation system).

Image on page 7: Getty Images

Printed and bound in the United States by Sheridan.

Distributed by Haymarket Books (www.haymarketbooks.org) to the trade in the U.S. through Consortium Book Sales and Distribution (www.cbsd.com) and internationally through Ingram Publisher Services International (www.ingramcontent.com).

To become a member, visit bostonreview.net/memberships.

For questions about donations and major gifts, contact Irina Costache, irina@bostonreview.net.

For questions about memberships, email members@bostonreview.net.

Boston Review
PO Box 390568
Cambridge, MA 02139

ISSN: 0734-2306 / ISBN: 978-1-946511-89-8

CONTENTS

Editors' Note   5

FORUM
We Need More Parties   7
Lee Drutman

*With responses from Danielle Allen, Deepak Bhargava & Arianna
Jiménez, Daniel Schlozman & Sam Rosenfeld, Josh Lerner,
Tabatha Abu El-Haj, Grant Tudor & Cerin Lindgrensavage,
Joel Rogers, Ian Shapiro, Bob Master, and Maurice Mitchell &
Doran Schrantz. Drutman replies.*

Post Colonialism | DISPATCH   95
Honora Spicer

The Dream of a Responsible Conservative | ESSAY   IOI
David Austin Walsh

Mapping Injury | INTERVIEW   II3
Sunaura Taylor interviewed by Rebecca Tuhus-Dubrow

The Politics of Price | REVIEW   127
Kevin P. Donovan

Inside Project 2025 | ESSAY   144
James Goodwin

Grieving in Rural America | REVIEW   159
Elizabeth Catte

CONTRIBUTORS   175

EDITORS' NOTE

AMERICAN POLITICS is more polarized than ever. In November we face another high-stakes election, pitting a fragile Democratic coalition against Donald Trump, who has said he will only be a dictator for the first day of his second term. How can we achieve a healthier democracy?

In our forum, Lee Drutman argues that we need to expand our two-party system. With just two major parties to choose from, lots of voters are pressured to stick with a team they do not like because the other side is far worse. Others are simply left out—casting their precious votes for third parties that can't win or withdrawing from politics altogether.

Drutman's solution is to revive *fusion voting*, an electoral system that allows different parties to nominate the same candidate for public office and run the candidate on their own ballot line. It was once the norm in U.S. politics, fostering a vibrant, multiparty political culture. But it started to be banned in the early twentieth century and remains legal today only in a handful of states. Bringing it back, Drutman urges, would empower new parties and give far more people a voice. This is a long-term project, but we can—we must—start now.

Can fusion be restored? Is it the best path to a more robust democracy? A range of reformers, organizers, and scholars weigh in, including former candidate for Massachusetts governor Danielle Allen, Working Families Party national director Maurice Mitchell, and New Party founder Joel Rogers. Most agree that democracy depends on strong parties. Some question how much fusion voting would help. Others propose different reforms or look to social movements as the primary drivers of change.

Also in this issue, contributors ask how public narratives advance or foreclose democratic possibilities. Honora Spicer reports from the U.S.-Mexico border, where a U.S. postal route was recently designated a national historic trail, eliding stories of exclusion hiding in plain sight. Kevin Donovan looks behind seemingly neutral accounting conventions, showing how they insulate political consequences from public debate.

And in a review of three new books, historian Elizabeth Catte dismantles political myths about poor and rural white people, clarifying who is responsible for their suffering and abandonment. She sees a way forward in Reverend William Barber's call for "moral fusion"—a movement built on bottom-up organization and solidarity among all those grieving in our broken democracy.

WE NEED MORE PARTIES

Lee Drutman

ROBERT F. KENNEDY JR. has no chance of becoming president, but he was not wrong when he said last fall that "Americans are angry at being left out, left behind, swindled, cheated, and belittled by a smug elite that has rigged the system in its favor." Fewer than one in four Americans think the country is heading in the right direction. More than two in three think the political and economic system needs major changes. Eight in ten are worried about the future of American democracy in the 2024 election. More than one in four view both parties unfavorably.

The stakes of this election are extremely high, but the pathologies of American politics will endure no matter the outcome. Antisystem alienation and hyperpartisanship are reinforcing each other in deeply destabilizing ways that can't be repaired simply by selecting better candidates.

We face a systemic problem that requires a systemic solution—and that solution, I contend, is to break out of our broken two-party system.

I make my case in two parts. The first explores how the U.S. party system lies at the root of our political dysfunction. The party system is the whole ballgame—it determines how citizens understand and engage in politics, the nature and tone of conflict, and the health and stability of democracy. When that system doesn't work properly, the politics that emerge from it will be broken, too—and other kinds of democratic reform will have only temporary impacts at best.

The way forward, I argue in the second part, is to introduce more parties and break the two-party doom loop, specifically by reviving *fusion voting*: an electoral system that allows multiple parties to endorse the same candidate for a public office. I say "revive" because fusion voting was once common in U.S. politics, before it was banned in the early twentieth century by the dominant parties. Though the state-by-state specifics varied, the broad motivation was simple: they didn't like all the added competition fusion enabled.

Today fusion voting remains legal only in two states, New York and Connecticut. Reviving it across the country would allow third parties to be legitimate players on the electoral scene—not just spoilers or bystanders. It would empower Americans who have long felt disillusioned with the two major parties—or disconnected from politics altogether—to have a real say. And it would pave the way to an important longer-term reform: proportional representation.

At this moment of hyperpartisanship, it may seem paradoxical to conclude that more parties are the solution. But modern representative democracy *is* party democracy; we need to make it work, not try to circumvent it. Reinvigorating the party system, with more and better parties, is the best place to start.

Part 1: It's the Party System, Stupid

THE RIGHT PRESCRIPTION to our ailing democracy depends on the right diagnosis, so it is important to get the story right about how we got to this moment.

The most common view is a classic decline-and-fall narrative. On this account, there was once a time when American democracy worked, before partisan polarization messed it all up. Moderates dominated; partisans disagreed, but they worked out differences in a spirit of constructive bipartisanship and remained close to the political center. This golden age allegedly peaked in the 1950s or early 1960s, and maybe even continued through the 1980s—but then things all went downhill starting in the 1990s with new confrontational politics pioneered by Newt Gingrich, the archetypical villain of this story. The tone in politics turned nasty and dysfunctional; cable news and talk radio, and then social media, destroyed everything. Most of the good, reasonable, compromise-minded politicians either left politics or got primaried by extremists.

This explanation is a good first approximation of what has gone wrong, and I have told versions of it in the past. But it oversimplifies in significant ways—and because it oversimplifies, it invites the wrong solution. If we want to fix things, this story suggests, we have to re-empower the "exhausted majority" in the middle—the mass of voters who just want stuff to get done, unlike the ideologues and extremists of left and right. In other words, we need to force parties to be more responsive to the "median voter."

Behind this metaphor of the "middle" lie several assumptions. One is that voters have consistent ideological preferences—formed independently of political parties—that can be specified on a single axis running from the extreme left to the extreme right. Another is that voters decide who to vote for by accurately selecting the party "closest" to them on this ideological spectrum—and that parties, too, can be classified in this one-dimensional way. Still another is that there really is a sizable group of voters in the political center.

When we talk in these terms, we are applying what political scientists call the "median voter theory" to American elections. And it's little surprise that we do so. As Jacob S. Hacker and Paul Pierson put it, this model has been the "master theory" of U.S. politics for half a century, at least among political scientists. Partly (but not only) for that reason, it is the analytical water in which much political analysis now swims.

The theory first came to prominence in Anthony Downs's 1957 book, *An Economic Theory of Democracy*. Having just finished a PhD in economics at Stanford, Downs deployed the tools of rational choice theory to explain why two-party politics might converge in the middle. It was not a crazy idea for the time. In the years following World War II, the two major parties *had* largely converged across a wide range of policy areas. Simultaneously, the academic study of politics was undergoing a sea change as a new generation of scholars embraced economic modeling for its apparent rigor. Unlike the thick methodologies of the field's

Drutman

past—which drew heavily on sociological and institutional theory—the new, "thin" models, it was argued, could be tested with data.

Both inside the academy and out, the median voter theory came to stand for an ideal as well as a natural state of politics. It provided a baseline against which commentators could analyze politics, campaign strategists could promote winning strategies, and political scientists could test hypotheses. A simplistic version flourished in the public sphere, offering a narrative that was both easy to understand and delightfully boosterish about the American two-party system. Array everyone on a single-axis line, assume most people are close to the middle, and voilà! You get an American success story: a stable two-party democracy of moderation and broad consensus.

In reality, Downs's argument hadn't been quite so simple. A two-party system "cannot provide stable and effective government," he wrote, "unless there is a large measure of ideological consensus among its citizens." This caveat proved prophetic. In September 1957 President Dwight Eisenhower federalized the National Guard in Little Rock, Arkansas, to protect nine Black teenagers who wished to attend Central High, which until then had been an all-white school. An angry white mob, backed by Governor Orval Faubus, showed up to prevent the teens from doing so. The background "consensus" that postwar U.S. politics had banked on suddenly seemed to dissolve—not least because it had depended on excluding a larger number of Americans from politics entirely, including African Americans in the Jim Crow South.

What median voter theorists had interpreted as two-party convergence along a one-dimensional axis was actually the result of a deeper, multidimensional process. Both parties had always contained multitudes—a mix of liberals, moderates, and conservatives of many types—and they competed with each other almost everywhere throughout the postwar era. We really had something like a hidden four-party system, with liberal Republicans and conservative Democrats alongside conservative Republicans and liberal Democrats. This factional diversity produced system-wide moderation: holding together the interests of multiple, overlapping groups prevented either of the two parties from swinging into extreme partisanship.

But this arrangement came under serious strain in the 1990s. As liberal Republicans and conservative Democrats began disappearing from Congress, U.S. politics became much more of a nonoverlapping two-party system. The result, as we all know now, has been disastrously divisive. The Democratic and Republican parties began to diverge, staking out increasingly distinct visions of American identity drawn from increasingly separated cultural and geographical bases.

Influential political analysts and reformers *should* have taken this divergence to mean that the median voter theory is wrong. Unfortunately, that hasn't happened. On the contrary, they have offered endless rationalizations for the gap between prediction and reality, and as a result median voter theory still gets prominent intellectual billing among columnists and mugwumps, who blame parties and partisanship for "distorting" politics. In doubling down on the one-dimensional "pulling apart" story, these commentators miss the real reason for the apparent disappearance of the political middle: the collapse of a de facto four-party system into a two-party system.

WHAT CAUSED this collapse? It started in the late 1960s with the rising salience of "social" issues around race, gender, and religion and the gradual disappearance of an older world of local party organizing. During the 1970s parties had only thin national networks—in which candidates could act relatively independently—but by the 1980s, the national apparatuses had grown financially stable and increasingly relied on consultants, ad makers, and ad buyers to shape their messages and candidates. Parties were thus transformed from local operations rooted in communities across the country into distant, national fund-raising juggernauts helmed by a professional political class. Today they bring in hundreds of millions of dollars each year—most of which goes straight to advertising and direct marketing.

Meanwhile, single-issue advocacy groups with strong policy views and financial backing began to proliferate and press their demands in Washington, and party leaders learned to arbitrage among them, shaping new coalitions by accumulating new stakes into politics. Business organizations became especially dominant. Starting in the 1990s, as politics became thoroughly nationalized around social and cultural issues, the country saw significant internal migration: Democrats abandoned rural and exurban areas, and Republicans abandoned urban areas. This geographic sorting in turn led to shrinking partisan competition in many areas—and the disappearance of party organizations along with it. After all, in a system of winner-take-all elections, why invest in places where support is below 40 percent? This geographic sorting atop single-winner districts was the central mechanism that drove the collapse of the de facto four-party system into only two parties.

In short, the two parties grew "hollow," in the apt phrasing of Daniel Schlozman and Sam Rosenfeld: they have come to be floating presences disconnected from most citizens, run by pollsters and messaging gurus. As a result, more and more citizens have become frustrated bystanders in national politics, and a growing share of citizens have rejected partisan conflict entirely. In some cases the major parties have responded by trying to fit more issues and groups in their coalitions, but mostly they have taken to demonizing the other side. You might not feel inspired by *us*, party leaders effectively tell voters, but *they* are terrible for the issues you care most about—abortion, as the Democrats emphasized, or religious "freedom," according to the GOP.

The cumulative effect of these changes has been disastrous. Partisan conflict is a blasted terrain, but voters who don't like it have nowhere to go. An overwhelming messaging machinery tells voters that even if they don't like their party, the other side winning would be far worse—and that losing, therefore, is unacceptable. It is under these conditions—high partisan division, low system legitimacy, high citizen disaffection—that democracies typically crumble.

If this is so, why aren't the critics of partisanship right? Their mistake is to see partisan polarization as the root cause of these ills. In fact, it is just a symptom of a significantly diminished partisan landscape. In modern representative democracies, partisan identity is not a distortion of some pre-partisan reality, and citizens are not the idealized, independent actors of rational choice models. On the contrary, study after study has shown that the vast majority of voters are partisans first: they derive their policy positions *from* the party they identify with, not the other way around. The more informed and engaged voters are, the more they know exactly what they should think as loyal partisans. The cleverer they are, the more they can reinterpret any fact pattern to explain why their party is right and the other party is wrong. More and better information—often proposed as a remedy to polarization—actually reinforces it.

To be a Democrat or a Republican (or a member of any party) means being part of a team, and when you see yourself as part of a team, you tend to be loyal to it. All of our collective identities—whether religious, ethnic, regional, or cultural—operate this way. We defend our teams when they are attacked, cheerlead when they succeed, and subscribe to the collective values that they promote. We look to our fellow group members to see what we should think about events in the world and update our views accordingly. We tend to self-segregate into the teams we want to be a part of—and when we don't see a team we want to be a part of, we sit things out.

These facts play out in perverse ways in our limited, two-party system. After January 6, for example, newly retired or defeated Republican members of Congress could have spoken up against Trump. Why didn't they? After all, they were no longer facing re-election. But with only two partisan "teams" to choose from, defection from the majority on your own side risks severe social isolation from friends and family and professional networks built up over years—a dark leap into harassment, loneliness, and professional demise.

In a recent interview in the *Atlantic*, former Representative Adam Kinzinger offered this explanation for why so many of his fellow Republicans went along with Trump: "I have come to learn that people fear losing their identity and losing their tribe more than they come to fear death." Of course, there is nothing special here about Republicans. Today our two major parties operate like super-powerful magnets, pulling and scaring people into their respective corners. Family background, historical memory, religion, geography, education, TV and social media viewing habits—all combine to keep us from straying to the other side, let alone creating a new side entirely.

In response to this state of affairs, many have proposed that we combat hyperpartisanship, perhaps by doing away with political parties entirely. Mickey Edwards, for example—a former Republican member of Congress—has argued that we should just view ourselves as Americans, not as members of a political team. Antipartisanship is the guiding principle behind No Labels, the organization Edwards cofounded that (as its name suggests) advocates for eschewing partisan labels.

But even "no label" is still a label; there is simply no escaping labels in politics. Moreover, there is little evidence that voters disillusioned with the two major parties are united in holding more or less the same centrist views. Most self-described "independents" are closet partisans, voting reliably for one party. (Many hold views even more extreme than partisans; they dislike parties because they see them as *too* compromise-oriented.) Similarly, "moderate" is the default category for people who don't identify as liberal or conservative—which doesn't mean that their views land in the metaphorical "middle" of the two camps. These two groups—self-identified independents and moderates—overlap somewhat, but the overlap is much smaller than critics of partisanship suggest. More than anything else, what holds them together is a sense that the system is broken.

This disconnect is a serious problem—in many ways even more serious than hyperpartisan polarization. According to surveys, political independents are least likely to embrace democratic values or even to support political compromise. This helps to explain why Trump's rise within the GOP in 2016 was powered by states with open primaries: he performed much better there than in states where only registered Republicans could vote for the party's nominee. Disconnection and apathy create a political opportunity for demagogues.

So much, then, for the mythical "middle." To connect citizens to politics, we must create more, and better, political parties—not seek to do away with parties altogether. New political parties provide a new identity: a new team that voters can join, a new way of seeing the world and belonging in it, and a new way of exercising power at the ballot box.

Of course, political parties are not the only "teams" that matter to politics. Labor unions are a powerful source of political identity (though less so, today, than they used to be). The same is true of many other civil society organizations. But because elections are the central institutions of modern representative democracy, political parties play a special role in organizing voting and governing power. They are "mega-identities," as political scientist Lilliana Mason describes them—and for that reason, there is no way around them.

Part 2: Getting Out of the Doom Loop

HOW DO WE make good on this vision of more and better parties? For starters, we can look to proportional, multiparty systems of the sort that are common in Europe.

In these systems, parties gain a share of legislative seats proportionate to their share of votes. In Sweden's 2022 general election, for example, a far-right political party—the Sweden Democrats—had its best showing ever, winning 20.5 percent of the vote. That means it got around 20.5 percent of the seats in the legislature. But because the Sweden Democrats did not win a majority, the party must bargain and form a coalition with other parties if it wishes to exercise power—an arrangement that limits its power considerably.

The legislative arm of the U.S. political system, by contrast, is built on winner-take-all congressional districts, which make it much easier for minorities to parlay victories into governing power. Take the MAGA faction of the U.S. Republican Party, defined as voters who believe that the 2020 election was stolen. It accounts for some 60 percent or more of people who voted for Trump in 2016 but only about 37 percent of all voters. Yet because it represents a majority of the GOP, the MAGA faction can convert its minority position across the United States into significant power. Moreover, in our climate of intense two-party polarization, many on the right who were originally reluctant to support the MAGA movement have thrown their lot in with it—since most find it more palatable to vote for a less-than-ideal GOP candidate than to vote for a Democrat.

More parties would make defections easier—without driving people out of politics altogether. What if we could empower non-MAGA Republicans and GOP-leaning independents to forge a distinct political identity, without asking them to waste their votes on a new third party that can't possibly win? Conversely, much of the self-identified left in the United States is deeply at odds with the Democratic Party, as well as with existing third parties. What if they could develop their own power base in electoral politics?

Fusion voting provides a powerful and proven answer. It was once common in U.S. politics, facilitating a vibrant political culture with many political parties. It can do so again.

Third Parties That Don't Spoil

IT'S NOT HARD to understand why third parties fail in our current party system: they are plagued by the "wasted" or "spoiler" vote problem. Voting for a minor-party candidate means voting for a candidate who simply cannot win. And in a close election, voting for a minor-party candidate could mean helping the candidate you least prefer. These facts make our third parties weak. Ambitious political actors channel all their energy into the major parties, while existing third parties attract only fringe candidates and donors.

Nevertheless, polls show widespread support for more than just two political parties. Gallup's most recent poll on this question found that 63 percent of Americans want "a third major party," a record high in twenty years of tracking.

Is there any hope for making this a reality? The one place where minor parties *aren't* weak are the states—New York and Connecticut—that still allow fusion voting. In both, the Working Families Party (WFP) is an independent and relevant actor in both elections and policy making, delivering votes to its major-party ally—some 8 percent of New Yorkers voted for Biden on the WFP line in 2020—while routinely demanding policy concessions for doing so. They don't win every election, and they don't get all their policy demands met, but they don't only lose, either. Non-fusion third parties always lose and thus cannot build power or agency. One might think of the WFP as an independent faction of the Democratic Party, but it's a faction with a ballot line, and that makes all the difference.

Consider what a fusion ballot could look like for a congressional office in a swing district where Democrats often poll head-to-head with Republicans. Say the Democratic Party nominates Smith, a moderate Democrat, while the Republican Party nominates Jones, a MAGA supporter. Suppose the Green Party and Libertarian Party nominate their own candidates, too.

So far, this is just like a typical ballot (at least in a place where third parties are active). But imagine there's a fifth, minor party in the mix, the Common Sense Party, with a base of moderates attracted to bipartisanship, civility, and the rule of law, and they decide to "fuse" with the Democrats for this race by cross-nominating the same candidate, Smith. For example, they might message to their base this way:

> We have evaluated the two major-party congressional candidates on their commitment to our values, and we're nominating Smith. She's a Democrat, and we disagree with the Democrats about many things, but on the values we care about, she's far and away best candidate in this race. If you agree these values are important, we urge you to vote for her under the Common Sense Party label. It counts the same as a vote on a major party line, but it lets her know that these values matter to you.

Election Day rolls around, and even though Smith gets fewer votes from Democrats than Jones does from Republicans, her support on the Common Sense line propels her to a narrow victory. The Common Sense Party can proudly claim to have produced the margin of victory. Smith will be most attentive to her own party, but she won't ignore Common Sense voters—and Republicans will be forced to run a more competitive candidate. In this scenario, supporters of the minor "fusion" party do not waste their votes (as supporters of the Green and Libertarian parties do). Instead, citizens vote for the candidate they prefer under the party label closest to their values.

At first glance, this scenario might seem unimportant. Business and civil society groups—unions, corporations, newspapers, organizations like the Democratic Socialists of America—already offer endorsements of major-party candidates without needing a ballot line. Why go through all the trouble of changing ballot rules and forging new political parties? One reason is that a place on the ballot organizes power in a distinct, tangible way. Votes get counted and can make or break elections; the impact of endorsements are much harder to quantify.

But there is an even more profound benefit to fusion voting than winning elections. As the Working Families Party has demonstrated, parties are essential mechanisms for giving citizens a meaningful voice, organizing power, and building political connections. This is the crucial value of political parties in modern representative democracy: they organize and cohere power at the ballot box, where it matters most. There is more to this vision than just endorsements from already existing civil society organizations. Endorsements can come and go and cannot easily be quantified; political parties are institutions that stick around from election to election. When voters choose to vote for a party, their power gets counted, and when organized power can be measured, it matters more.

Everything Old Is New Again

IT IS NOT just the present that we can turn to for inspiration. Though largely forgotten outside New York and Connecticut, fusion is a key part of U.S. history. It was widely used in the nineteenth century, where it created space for new parties to form and elevate issues the major parties preferred to ignore.

In the decades before the Civil War, for example, the abolitionists used many tactics to elevate their opposition to slavery: massive petitions, public assemblies, protecting fugitives from slave catchers, and much more. But before long, it was clear that they had to be involved in politics, so the abolitionists formed antislavery political parties, among them the Liberty Party, the Anti-Nebraska Party, and the Free Soil Party. Where it was possible to win a stand-alone election for, say, a Free Soil candidate, abolitionists embraced that choice. But where it wasn't, they used fusion voting brilliantly. In effect, they said to their supporters:

> We are backing Hiram Ebenezer Smith, even though we know he is a Whig who is not perfect on abolition, because he's far better than his proslavery Democratic opponent, Ezekiel Frederick Jones. So vote for Smith, but do so on the Liberty Party ticket and let him know he must stand up against the Slave Power.

Among the most famous abolitionists in Congress, and by some reckonings the greatest of all U.S. senators, was Charles Sumner of Massachusetts. He was elected due to the unusual fusion coalition of Free Soil and Democratic state legislators in what was then an indirect election.

Due in no small part to abolitionists' fusion voting efforts, the Whig Party collapsed in 1854 (ending a twenty-year run), and a new major party—the Republican Party—was created on the foundation laid by the Liberty, Free Soil, Anti-Nebraska, Know-Nothings, Know-Somethings, and other abolitionist political actors. As historian Corey Brooks writes, this was "the most important third-party movement in American history."

After the Civil War, fusion balloting expanded across the nation. For decades Americans had a vigorous, multiparty system in which citizens who felt their interests were being disregarded by the two major parties could—and did—build minor parties. These parties, bolstered by the ability to tie their interests to major parties through fusion voting, became important voices in the public square: farmers' parties, labor parties, temperance parties, suffragist parties, debtor parties, Black parties, and more.

The most famous was the coalition of farmers and tradesmen known as the People's Party, or Populists. In North Carolina in the 1890s, white yeoman farmers voting for the Populists united with emancipated slaves who voted Republican to elect a multiracial slate of officeholders. They had separate organizations and vastly different cultures and history, but the state's fusion voting rules allowed them to support the same candidates, producing a coalition victory. The fact that this arrangement was later destroyed by Klan violence and Jim Crow Democrats who soon banned fusion voting only underscores how valuable these rules are.

So What Happened to Fusion Voting?

IN THE LATE nineteenth century, state governments took over the printing of standardized, so-called "Australian" ballots. Before then, parties had printed and distributed their own ballots to supporters that listed the favored candidates (and only those candidates) or published them in party newspapers for voters to cut out and bring to polling places.

The Australian ballot had much to recommend it: it resulted in less fraud, and it protected the right of voters to keep their votes a secret. But it didn't take long for the dominant parties to realize that if the state controlled the printing of ballots, the party that controlled the state could introduce rules to favor its own interests. Since fusion typically results in an alliance between a minor party and the weaker of the two major parties, the dominant major party in a state or region—in the North the Gilded Age Republicans, in the South the Jim Crow Democrats—had every incentive to prevent such alliances.

Those interests were made crystal clear in one of the earliest state legislative debates about banning fusion. Summarizing his reasons for wanting to outlaw the alliance between Democrats and Populists (or Prohibitionists), the Republican Speaker of the Michigan Assembly in 1898 put it this way: "We can whip them single-handed, but don't intend to fight all creation." As historian Peter Argersinger puts it, the Republicans' solution was a form of "ballot manipulation"—strategically altering election laws or practices by a political party to undermine the effectiveness of opposing parties' electoral coalitions. The fusion ban passed and was soon followed by a raft of similar legislation. By the early 1920s most states had passed copycat fusion bans, though a few states only came around later. And with fusion outlawed, minor parties had no good options: they could run a standalone candidate that would not be viable, or they bite the bullet, discard the party's distinctive identity, and join one of the major parties.

As a result, the United States is the only developed nation in the world that did not see the emergence of a meaningful new national political party in the twentieth century. Ironically—and tragically—the very system that allowed the Republican Party to develop a real alternative to the incumbent parties that were failing the nation in the 1850s is no longer available.

By recovering the dynamic, multiparty strain of U.S. history, we can see the larger story of American democracy: a story of a diverse array of parties rising, fusing, falling, shifting. The language of a one-dimensional political spectrum didn't enter American political discussions until the 1930s, when third parties fully faded from the scene and Democrats and Republicans truly became dominant, leaving the United States a genuinely two-party system—but with parties that still contained multitudes within them. As U.S. politics nationalized and hyperpolarized in the 1980s and 1990s, the two parties flattened out—leaving us with the destructive system we have today.

HOW COULD we get fusion back? Congress could pass legislation tomorrow making it legal for all congressional elections. State legislatures could pass legislation for statewide elections. Ballot initiatives could relegalize fusion. But the most likely immediate pathway is through state-based litigation. Because fusion was once widely legal, and because many state constitutions lay emphasis on freedom of association, litigation offers a direct path to reviving fusion voting in many states. Already, lawsuits in New Jersey and Kansas are in progress; other states will follow soon.

Of course, it will take time for more and better parties to form and flourish—to recruit members, organize an agenda, and build power. And fusion voting is by no means the only structural reform that we need in the United States. Public campaign financing would help to check the profound influence of a small number of very wealthy donors, and in the long term, proportional representation would support a robust and representative multiparty system capable of representing America's pluralism and diversity.

But the bottom line is that there is no nonpartisan "state of political nature" to which we can return. American politics is not in crisis because of too much partisanship but, in a sense, because of too little. Multiple, vibrant political parties are the only way to organize power in modern democracies, and if we don't change the party system we have, the two-party doom loop will only grow worse. Fusion voting plots a clear path out—it hits the sweet spot where impact and feasibility meet, and it is long past time to revive it.

FORGET FUSION, LOOK TO ALASKA!

Danielle Allen

TO BLAME OUR current party system for the dysfunction of our democracy is not to argue that we would be better off without parties. As Drutman says, reinvigorating our party system is "the only path forward."

Drutman also rightly argues that we should reform the laws governing parties if we want to increase political dynamism. But he is wrong to think that fusion voting will bring back that dynamism or create multipartyism.

The heady, mid-nineteenth-century period of party politics that Drutman admires was the product of an era when parties were un-regulated, private entities. The problem with our party politics today isn't that fusion ended. The problem is that the party apparatus was co-opted by the state around the same time.

As Drutman points out, states began to ban fusion voting in the late nineteenth century after they took on responsibility for printing ballots. No longer would parties send voters into the booth with tickets printed by their parties; instead, candidates' names would now be printed on one public ballot, which voters could use to keep their vote secret. But just as states took responsibility for running the general election with the use of unified ballots, they also began to take responsibility for running party primaries. Starting in the early twentieth century, taxpayer dollars were committed to funding primaries that selected the candidates from each party who would appear on the unified ballot in the general election.

But public money always comes with strings. Along with taxpayer funding came new state requirements about what it takes to form a party. In the early nineteenth century, parties formed simply by organizing; groups of people came together to develop and execute a shared agenda. With early twentieth-century reforms, states began to require that parties meet certain criteria—through signature gathering and party conventions, charters, and platforms—to gain the right to place a candidate on the ballot. States also introduced a minimum number of votes required to maintain status as a party.

In other words, running a party became a state-regulated activity—and diverse rules proliferated around the country. The rules significantly raised the barrier to entry for new parties, and the diversity of rules across states made matters even worse. In order to function nationally, parties today have to master fifty different sets of procedures. Even though the Libertarian Party was founded in 1971, it did not achieve ballot access in all fifty states until 1980, and it has not maintained that access consistently, achieving it again only in 1992, 1996, 2016, and 2020. The Green Party, founded in 1984, has thus far maxed out at forty-four states.

Fusion voting simply cannot solve this problem: the difficulty of getting a range of candidates on the ballot in the first place. Indeed, fusion voting seems to make very little difference even where it does exist. Consider the Working Families Party in New York. In 2000 the party claimed roughly 0.07 percent of registered voters. This year, after nearly a quarter-century of effort, it represents about 0.42 percent. Over the same period, the share of Democrats grew from 46 to about 49 percent. This is not favorable evidence that fusion will promote party dynamism.

A better reform would use taxpayer dollars only for public functions—like keeping our votes confidential—while returning to parties the functions that should be the responsibility of civil society associations, like selecting their standard bearer. Alaska's new election system, passed in 2020 and first implemented in 2022, does just that.

In particular, the state now runs just one, unified primary. Instead of requiring candidates to go through a party process to get their names on the ballot, the ballot includes everyone who meets certain requirements established by state law and that vary by office (typically, the gathering of a sufficient number of signatures or the paying of a fee). All candidates can choose to be identified by the label of the party with which they affiliate as a way of providing voters with information about their positions. Meanwhile, parties can still hold conventions and endorse a candidate—and the endorsement will show up on the ballot—and they are fully responsible for funding that process. Parties also cannot block candidates who affiliate with them but aren't endorsed, provided those candidates have met the state's requirement for ballot access.

The result is an all-candidates primary on a unified ballot. If four or fewer candidates qualify for ballot access, the primary is canceled, and all candidates move on to the general election. If more than four qualify, voters pick the one candidate they prefer, and the four candidates who win the greatest number of votes move forward to an instant runoff in the general election, where ranked choice voting is used to ensure a majority winner. In the general, voters are invited, but not required, to vote not only for a first choice but also for a second and third. This structure is important; since it enables voters to select backups, third-party candidates can maximize their vote share. This method should quickly make third-party strength visible as it starts to grow, which in turn will draw media attention and create a positive feedback loop that will enhance public learning. That should make it possible for third parties to establish their footing better.

This kind of reform is necessary and urgent, and other states should follow Alaska's lead. But by itself, it won't restore the system-wide dynamism that Drutman advocates. We also need to change the rules that determine when an organization has earned the status of a political party and can put a candidate on the public ballot.

That will be much harder, but I think Drutman is right when he says that we should focus on the sweet spot where impact and feasibility meet. Right now, that is democracy, Alaska-style.

THE REAL ENGINE OF CHANGE
Deepak Bhargava & Arianna Jiménez

DRUTMAN IS partly right: the "two-party doom loop" threatens American democracy and structural reform is needed. But his framework can't explain how authoritarian movements have seized governing power in countries with multiparty systems such as India, Hungary, and Brazil, and it misses part of the American story. Fusion voting in a multiparty system would provide a big boost in the fight against authoritarianism, but it is not a silver bullet.

Indeed, there are multiple causes of the crisis we face. Our system of government has many deeply undemocratic features baked in by design: the Electoral College, the Senate, and a Supreme Court subject to political capture, to name only a few. Rooted in slavery and elite fear of mass participation in politics, these arrangements block the wills of majorities from being reflected in policy on a wide range of issues, from reproductive rights to gun control to climate change.

This system has not prevented the rise of grotesque economic inequality or the stagnation of living standards for majorities, who increasingly view politics as a spectacle disconnected from their daily lives. Members of both parties have been complicit in this titanic failure of democratic governance over the last fifty years—by supporting tax cuts for the wealthy, the deregulation of corporations, and an evisceration of the social safety net. These conditions, in turn, have fueled the rise of populist, authoritarian movements, which weaken key pillars of democracy, from voting rights to the right to peaceful protest. Their emergence is not only the result of elite manipulation or a failure of political structures (though these factors are certainly accelerants); economic and social conditions are central.

Perhaps the most important cause of our democratic crisis is the collapse of civil society organizations: the churches, unions, and community groups that bring together large numbers of people. Without them, democracy cannot flourish—no matter how much voting mechanisms are reformed.

Neoliberalism has atomized us. Authoritarian movements thrive on the disconnection, apathy, fear, and anxiety that now characterize our individual lives and our culture. The culture of neoliberalism fosters hyperindividualism, blames people who don't get rich for their failure to do so, and undermines solidarity. In an advisory issued last year, the Surgeon General warned of an "epidemic of loneliness and isolation." In 2018, only 16 percent of Americans reported feeling "very attached to their local community." The advisory also cites a decrease in involvement in civic organizations, including "religious groups, clubs, and labor unions."

The weakening of unions—a core strategy of neoliberal governance—is a particularly important and insufficiently appreciated driver of authoritarianism. As political scientists Jake Grumbach and Ruth Berins Collier have argued in these pages,

> unions were critical in sustaining mass democracy by virtue of their role in organizing, mobilizing, and sustaining a politics that embraced a broad pro-democratic coalition, which they were able to do on the basis of materialist demands that went beyond the specific interests of their own membership.

The upshot is clear. Participation in membership organizations is crucial to a healthy democracy, providing important ways for people to build connections, get to know their colleagues or neighbors, and feel part of something bigger than themselves. If democracy doesn't exist in your neighborhood or workplace—and if the habits of democracy aren't practiced in your union or local community organizations—it's unlikely to be persuasive for you as a system of organizing society. It's no wonder that a record-low percentage of Americans feel "satisfied with the way democracy is working."

Though Drutman acknowledges the role of civil society organizations, he passes over them too quickly, downplaying their significance in light of the "mega-identities" that he says parties help to construct. But can we build those "mega-identities" in the absence of organizations that cultivate people's identities as workers or ground their attachments to place or shared faith? The evidence from successful anti-authoritarian movements around the world suggests not. The Workers Party in Brazil, for example, is nourished by its roots in unions and organizations of landless workers, women, Afro-Brazilians, and LGBTQ+ people.

Bhargava & Jiménez

Such organizations have played an essential role in nourishing democracy in the United States too. The great expansions of democracy in U.S. history, from the abolition of slavery to the expansion of the right to vote for women and African Americans, were brought about by vibrant social movements, rooted in organizations like the Black church, suffragette groups, and labor unions. At times, multiparty structures have helped achieve reforms, as Drutman suggests. But the engine of change has always been mass participation in social movements, which provide the momentum to overcome daunting barriers in the structures of politics—as when the civil rights movement forced change through a Senate held captive by leaders from states of the former Confederacy.

While an authoritarian threat now looms and civil society has been diminished, the upsurge of worker organizing in recent years offers a source of enormous hope. In the past year alone, Volkswagen workers in Chattanooga voted to join the United Auto Workers, becoming the first in the South to do so at a company outside of the Big Three (Ford, GM, and Chrysler). Meanwhile, fast food workers in California have established the first-ever union for the industry, and public support for unions continues to grow. According to a recent Pew poll, 54 percent of U.S. adults believe the decline in union membership has been "bad for the country," and 59 percent say it has been "bad for working people."

Along with unions, a new generation of community and faith-based organizations are working in rural areas and with constituencies too often neglected by progressives. Tackling issues from the opioid crisis to child and family well-being, organizations like Hoosier Action in Indiana and ISAIAH in Minnesota are restoring people's sense of agency, bringing people across lines that often divide us, and creating a sense of belonging in this era of radical isolation.

In stark contrast to the bottom-up mass movements that have driven most advances in American democracy, the field of democracy advocates in the United States has been disproportionately white and middle-class, focused on top-down, technocratic reforms to political systems—many of which are promising, but lack a mass base connected to working-class people. The reality is that a strong democracy requires not just a healthy electoral system, but also a rich ecosystem of civil society organizations that bring people from different backgrounds together and invite them to imagine a better future.

Electoral reforms, including fusion voting, can certainly help drive democratic revival. In fact, one of the strongest cases for fusion voting is one that Drutman doesn't make: it can work synergistically with community and labor organizing, by incentivizing community organizations to build political organizations that more directly bring their members' voices into the democratic arena. Likewise, broader structural reform must surely be part of how we unrig a system that fails working-class people. But there can be no shortcuts to building the mass organizations and movements that will power a democratic resurgence.

Bhargava & Jiménez

POWER, NOT PROCESS

Daniel Schlozman & Sam Rosenfeld

DRUTMAN IS a rarity in American politics: a process-oriented reformer who is also a cheerleader for political parties. Ever since the Gilded Age, reformers aiming to fiddle with rules, clean up politics, and make it less nasty have tended to be anti-party. In their eyes, parties and party politicians divide society and foment needless anger.

Drutman deserves great credit for rejecting this outlook. Nevertheless, his vision of pro-party reform retains a distinctly limited character. We take our cue from a very different tradition of pro-party reform that emphasizes how parties serve as vehicles for social visions. Most notably, midcentury liberals sought a Democratic Party that would fulfill the New Deal's promise. Procedural reform, in this tradition, is inseparable from its substantive ends.

In that spirit, we worry that Drutman overpromises and underdelivers. We find both his diagnosis ("hyperpartisanship") and his proposed cure (fusion voting) hindered by a view of parties as creators of identities rather than as claimants for power. And we find his analysis obtuse to the partisan and institutional sources of our present predicament. Today's threats to American democracy emerge largely from the right, and they interact with the deep flaws in a Madisonian system that frustrates majorities— but Drutman is too shy about the former fact and too neglectful of the latter. We see value in throwing anti-Trump Republicans the lifeline of a ballot line, one that also teaches centrists worried about democracy to appreciate the merits of party. But we must be clear-eyed about its limits as a solution.

Consider the institutional perils first. Yale political scientist Juan Linz warned in 1990 of "the perils of presidentialism," with its zero-sum conflict and its temptations toward demagogy. At the time, Linz wasn't concerned about the seemingly stable United States. Yet this country now exhibits virtually all the pathologies he described, with high-pitched presidential elections refracted through the rickety Electoral College. The wildly unrepresentative Senate stands out among the world's legislatures as a sorry outlier. Frequent periods of divided government, to say nothing of the Senate's extraconstitutional supermajority rules for cloture, make for gridlock and stalemate. And a Supreme Court with extremely strong judicial review and life tenure for its members has anointed itself as the system's ultimate decider.

Meanwhile, the Republican Party has become decidedly dangerous. The trouble runs far deeper than mere polarization: all-consuming resentment politics, careening short-termism, institutional ruthlessness, and shameless embrace of ethnonationalism. These

Schlozman & Rosenfeld

tendencies trace back decades in American conservatism; the separation between mainstream and extreme right imagined by many now-disillusioned conservatives is largely a myth. By 2016, it took only Donald Trump's match to ignite the dumpster fire. One can find examples of destructive and even antisystem behavior on the other side aplenty, but *as a party*, the problem is the Republicans, and any diagnosis ought to proceed accordingly.

These institutional and partisan ills have become inseparable. As Steven Levitsky and Daniel Ziblatt have noted, the GOP has turned away from even the attempt to win big popular majorities as rural biases in the political system give the party a leg up. Its efforts to exploit the rules of the game now extend not just to districting and voter eligibility but the counting of votes. And, as the events of January 6, 2021, made all too vivid, Republicans increasingly disavow the willingness to lose and fight again that stands at the very core of democracy. Tackling these linked crises means thinking about party projects to win majorities and wield state power in ways that will vanquish the appeal of Trumpism. And it means institutional reform that will attack the system's weak points head on. If either or both of those goals are deemed wrong or impossible, fair enough. But these substantive stakes ought to inform democracy promoters' conversations about solutions.

From this perspective, fusion's weaknesses come to the fore. Most immediately, fusion does nothing about presidentialism, never mind the Senate and the Supreme Court. No matter how votes accrue, only one person will serve as president. Fusion thus offers no way out from the high-stakes drama of presidential elections or the president's temptations to arrogate power in office. As scholars of Latin American politics have stressed time and again, multipartyism and presidentialism are a bad mix, making coalitions hard to build and opposition hard to coalesce.

What fusion does offer, appealingly, is a way for pro-democracy forces unhappy with waving the Democratic banner to join a multiparty coalition during our (lowercase) democratic emergency. From the left, the plucky Working Families Party (WFP) in New York has long extolled the mechanism. In turn, Drutman has helped to raise fusion's profile among centrist reformers. But beyond these two pockets, it is hard to see where the energy for fusion will come from or why fusion hits the "sweet spot"—at once achievable and transformative—that Drutman claims for it. Perhaps mainstream Democrats and some substantial number of Republicans will see the logic and join the charge, but Drutman does not explain just how this might happen.

Fusion's history illuminates its limits. It was a component but hardly the linchpin of a complex, now-vanished nineteenth-century political system. Party politics, in the antebellum period especially, was fluid, with loyalties shifting and new parties forming and break-ing apart. Parties were often meant as temporary expedients rather than permanent institutions, and separate state organizations came together only in the quadrennial national convention. Those parties would often cross-endorse, but such endorsements were contingent responses to particular situations, not an inevitability of the process. Contrary to Drutman's claims, the sectarian Liberty Party refused to support even Joshua Giddings, the most radical antislavery Whig in the House. Nor did the collapse of the Whig Party emerge in any direct way from "abolitionists' fusion-voting efforts." Fusion could not then and cannot now reorient the fundamental patterns of division in national politics.

Fusion's more recent fate in New York also offers only tempered grounds for optimism. WFP has often been a valuable player, but its preeminent concern with its own ballot line, for which it must receive 130,000 votes for president or governor, has weakened its substantive contribution. The ballot line itself, more than any policy, was the central element in the long, convoluted drama between WFP and its archnemesis, Andrew Cuomo. And before it, the Liberal Party, initially a vehicle for labor unions' anticommunist reform politics, devolved into a patronage mill that wags deemed neither liberal nor a party. Fusion has hardly fostered an ideal political culture surrounding it. New York has restrictive rules around voting and elections, and the dominant New York Democratic Party is notably dysfunctional.

An unacknowledged tension runs through Drutman's argument. On the one hand, he appreciates parties for their staying power as "the clans of electoral politics," offering "belonging and purpose." On the other hand, he suggests parties can arise quickly, at just the right moment, when circumstances—like ours now—require. This view softens the institutional demands of party and the special meaning of party loyalty. As Drutman rightly says, there is more to parties than "endorsements from already existing civil society organizations." Define party downward and it risks becoming just an NGO with a ballot line.

At a time when the two parties are stretched to the breaking point, some kind of relief valve looks mighty appealing. But being pro-party means more than multiplying ballot lines. It means building a polity with the "organized power" of robust parties at the very core.

BEYOND ELECTIONS

Josh Lerner

ELECTIONS HAVE BECOME nearly synonymous with democracy. We invest so much hope, energy, and money in elections and keep ending up with out-of-touch politicians, legislative gridlock, and violent polarization. Even if our candidate wins, the broken system remains. And yet, we have trouble imagining what else democracy might be. We keep searching for magical electoral solutions, whether voting for a savior or electoral reform, but we rarely think about the terrain beyond elections.

Drutman correctly observes that our party and electoral systems are broken. He proposes a smart electoral reform: fusion voting. I'm fortunate to live in New York, where fusion voting is relatively established. It's wonderful, letting voters more clearly express our political beliefs. But Drutman goes astray in claiming that a single reform is *the* systemic solution. This is the same "solutionism" that plagues the technology and media sectors—the "to save everything, click here" gambit, as Evgeny Morozov puts it.

Systemic solutions to our democratic ills require a much broader approach beyond elections. We certainly need to defend and improve electoral systems, but a single-minded focus on elections is itself part of our democratic malaise. Most people don't believe that elections are delivering actual democracy—government by and for the people—and they're right.

Of course, it may seem foolish to say we should focus less on elections, especially with so many critical elections happening now. But we say the same thing every couple of years. There are alternatives. Cities and countries around the globe have used practices of participatory, deliberative, and direct democracy, alongside elections, to enable government by and for the people. We need to stop obsessing over one single flawed aspect of democracy and embrace different ways for people to decide different issues in different contexts. The only solution is many solutions. And to understand these solutions, we need to reckon with a deeper problem.

The fundamental problem is that throughout history, elections have generally not resulted in genuine democracy. As the work of scholars like Martin Gilens and Benjamin Page has shown, elected representative government has given economic elites and business groups oversized political influence, while average citizens have little or no influence. This is oligarchy, not democracy. Even worse, elections have tended to attract and put in power people who are more narcissistic and psychopathic than average.

Most people also hate how electoral democracy works. According to the Pew Research Center, most people in electoral democracies say that "their political system needs major changes or needs to be completely reformed." In the United States, a majority across nearly all demographic groups and ideologies believe that the country's system of government does not work. People around the world agree: only 17 percent consider U.S. democracy a good model.

Even in places that have adopted powerful electoral reforms like mandatory voting, proportional representation, and remote voting, such as Brazil and Australia, trust in democracy is declining, polarization is rising, and people are increasingly rejecting government institutions. The moral is that electoral reform is necessary but insufficient.

This argument dates back to ancient Athens, whose citizens found that elections ended up benefiting elites and preventing government by the people. To prevent rule by the elite or the most charismatic, Athenians set up additional ways for the people to govern. They designed an ingenious alternative to voting for representatives: lotteries. As with modern-day juries, any Athenian citizen could be randomly selected to serve on the city's governing councils. At the same time, Athens enabled direct citizen voting on policies, through a broader "popular assembly." This combination of voting, lotteries, and direct participation is the bold system that the word "democracy" originally denoted. Athenian democracy was far from perfect, of course; many people—women, enslaved people, and others—were excluded from citizenship. But the basic idea of resisting rule by the elite was a good one.

Over the last few decades, the "lottery" approach to democracy has started to make a comeback through a wave of deliberative democracy. Since the 1980s, over six hundred lottery-based democracy initiatives have launched around the world. These programs convene a randomly selected but representative sample of the public to learn about an issue and identify solutions. They have contributed to major policy changes, such as overturning Ireland's ban on abortion.

As an alternative to selecting representatives, citizens have also voted directly on policies and laws, through direct democracy. Historically, this first meant face-to-face assemblies, such as town hall meetings in the United States. Many cities, states, and nations have invited citizens to vote on policies at a larger scale, through ballot initiatives, measures, or referendums, such as votes on abortion regulation or animal rights in the United States or on environmental protection and marriage equality in Taiwan.

Governments have also used participatory democracy to enable people to decide policies, laws, and budgets, by mixing methods of representative, deliberative, and direct democracy. Participatory budgeting is the most widespread example, letting citizens decide how to spend public budgets in over seven thousand governments around the world. Community members propose and discuss spending ideas, then vote to decide which ones to fund. The winning proposals are then implemented by the government.

Moreover, many cities and countries are experimenting with weaving together these democratic practices, to build stronger ecosystems of democracy. In 2021 Paris's City Council created a permanent citizens' assembly, a randomly selected body of citizens with real governing power. Among other roles, the citizens' assembly picks the annual theme for the city's participatory budgeting program, which lets residents decide how to spend €100 million each year. Participatory budgeting, the citizens' assembly, and city council are stronger together.

South Korea has scaled up this approach. Its national participatory budgeting program, My Budget, combines participatory, deliberative, direct, and representative democracy. Citizens submit, discuss, and prioritize programs. The government then screens them for feasibility and sends them to a randomly selected Citizens' Budget Committee. It discusses and prioritizes the proposals, and the government includes them in the national budget. In 2021, 63 proposals were funded, with around $86 million—a relatively small amount measured against the nation's total budget, but a microcosm of what's possible.

These programs begin to show what a more functional democracy might look like. They effectively let ordinary people—not just elected politicians—decide policies, laws, and budgets. But these are baby steps. Meanwhile, another global movement is making giant strides in a different direction, turning democracy into oligarchy.

The greatest threat to democracy is not our broken party system—it's the surging movement against democracy. Billionaires and autocrats are bankrolling a global network of think tanks, universities, media, hackers, activists, and lobbyists to prevent government by the people, as Jane Mayer and Nancy MacLean have documented. They are funding efforts to sow division and distrust, prevent people from voting, overturn election results, and downsize government. Even the minimalist democracy of elections is a threat to oligarchs' accumulation of wealth and power.

When antidemocratic movements attack elections, our natural response is to defend elections. But in doing so, we opt into the discussion that antidemocratic forces want to have, in one of the few areas where they enjoy popular support: "Elections aren't working so well, are they?"

Rather than just defending elections, it's time to advance a bolder vision of democracy. Antidemocratic movements have won support by calling for a radical transformation of government. It's time for pro-democracy movements to counter with an equally ambitious transformation, from a dysfunctional system dominated by elections to a healthy ecosystem of diverse democratic practices. It's time to get over our obsession with elections, to win the democracy that we deserve.

A MODEST PROPOSAL
Tabatha Abu El-Haj

THE MEASURE OF any reform proposal is twofold. Is it a good idea, and is it possible?

Drutman's call to restore fusion is both. It is a good idea because it is a party-centric reform with real potential to leverage meaningful democratic returns. We must reconcile ourselves to this core idea: "Modern representative democracy *is* party democracy." There is no way out of the party system, but this does not mean that it couldn't be better. Our contemporary party system is broken both because it is nationalized and because it only has space for two sides. Fusion politics offers a promising path out of this "doom loop." When third parties can only act as spoilers, their electoral appeal is limited, and they have no incentive to be serious. Allow them a real seat at the table and they will do the associative work of a party, connecting citizens to the government, building power, and delivering legislative goods by negotiating deals.

Restoring fusion is also a refreshingly modest reform. Unlike proposals to abolish the Electoral College or permit the regulation of money in politics, it does not require a constitutional amendment. It also does not require Americans to look to Congress, and no one will need to be educated about how votes are counted, or seats apportioned in proportional systems. Perhaps most importantly, a narrow path to the relegalization of fusion exists. Restoring fusion politics requires only minimal amendments to existing state election laws. The two most significant obstacles are legislative self-interest and the Supreme Court's 1997 decision in *Timmons v. Twin Cities Area New Party*. Consider each in turn.

All reform proposals must account for the fact that current officeholders are just not reliable partners when it comes to meaningful democratic reforms; their first instinct is to fortify their political power. Anti-fusion laws are a case in point. The very first anti-fusion law, passed in South Dakota in 1893, was a Republican-led legislative effort. Seeking to thwart the electoral threat posed by political alliances between Democrats and Populists, Republican legislatures around the country soon followed suit. State legislatures, controlled by the two major parties, will have little incentive to reinstitute fusion.

There have been important exceptions—occasions when partisan incentives have aligned with the interest of democratic reform. In 2007 the Democratic-led Connecticut legislature amended the state's cross-nomination rules to make fusion functionally usable. Before the change, the state allowed only "major parties" (a legal status) to fuse, imposing cumbersome rules for "minor parties" seeking to do the same. The rules were relaxed largely in response to the emergence of the Working Families Party (WFP), despite the cumbersome rules. The WFP had the support of many of the state's largest labor unions and generally preferred to cross-endorse major party candidates who embraced its policy goals. In Connecticut's competitive districts, candidates cross-endorsed by the WFP were overwhelmingly Democrats.

One result was that the WFP was able to cross-endorse Democrat Dan Malloy in the 2010 governor's race. The votes Malloy received on the WFP line far exceeded his narrow margin of victory. Malloy strongly supported the WFP's top legislative priority—paid sick days—and in 2011 Connecticut became the first state to guarantee paid sick days to workers.

Trump's bid for a second term may create a similar political opening; the interests of the old guard of the Republican Party and the Democrats may converge to reintroduce fusion legislatively. Alternatively, one party may decide to embrace fusion in response to evidence suggesting the real possibility of partisan realignment.

But I wouldn't bet on it. The more likely scenario is that of Minnesota. In 1994, the newly formed Twin Cities Area New Party, a coalition of labor unions and community organizers, sought to repeal Minnesota's ban on fusion with the help of its ally and future nominee, Andy Dawkins, a much-loved incumbent state representative. Representing the Democratic-Farmer-Labor Party (DFL), Dawkins sponsored a bill to relegalize fusion and introduce weekend voting, but the bill was killed in committee. Incumbents from the two major parties worried that striking the state's ban on fusion would weaken their hold on power.

The classic solution to this conundrum is to turn to the courts. As Justice Harlan Stone suggested in 1938, the power of judicial review is precisely suited to situations where the law makes it difficult to "repeal . . . undesirable legislation" or oust unpopular elected officials. The Warren Court fully embraced this idea, viewing the Court's primary role in our system of checks and balances as reinforcing the openness of the democratic process.

In 1996 the Twin Cities Area New Party tried to make such an appeal to the courts. The case arose when the party formally nominated Dawkins, who represented a multiracial working-class district that benefitted little from Bill Clinton's Third Way policies and was keen on the cross-nomination. The secretary of state of Minnesota rejected it. The New Party sued, confident that the federal courts would strike down Minnesota's ban on fusion candidacies as an infringement on a fair political process. It lost.

In a widely criticized decision, a divided Supreme Court upheld Minnesota's anti-fusion law, maintaining that it did not severely burden the New Party's First Amendment rights. The party, it insisted, remained free to nominate an alternative, eligible candidate for the office *or* to electioneer on behalf of its preferred candidate under the DFL banner. The Court resoundingly rejected the New Party's argument that "Minnesota's interest in maintaining a stable political system . . . [did] not give the state license to frustrate consensual political alliances." Instead, it asserted that whatever burdens the law might place on the New Party were justified by the Minnesota legislature's view that "political stability is best served through a healthy two-party system."

The ruling remains a significant obstacle to a federal judicial path to relegalizing fusion. But it does not bind state courts, and many state constitutions provide broad protections for free and fair elections. Advocates of fusion in recent years have seized this narrow opportunity and instituted a state constitutional litigation strategy.

The first of these suits was filed in New Jersey. It makes an affirmative state constitutional case for striking down New Jersey's, particularly burdensome law while also offering numerous reasons to reject the U.S. Supreme Court's reasoning in *Timmons*. (Like several other legal academics, I participated in the New Jersey case as an amicus, highlighting errors in the *Timmons* ruling's First Amendment analysis.) These state constitutional lawsuits are promising and likely critical to a successful effort to reintroduce fusion.

Political change is difficult. It requires reformers to find and exploit limited opportunities within an array of structural constraints—political and legal. It should surprise no one that the opportunities for revitalizing fusion politics are severely constrained. However narrow the path, the critical point is that the prospects for reviving fusion politics are far more promising than many of the alternatives currently under consideration.

A PATH TO MULTIPLE PARTIES

Grant Tudor & Cerin Lindgrensavage

DRUTMAN IS NOT alone in his diagnosis of the problem with American democracy: that most roads, if you follow them long enough, lead back to the two-party system. Research has linked the system to a list of maladies: hyperpolarization, inept governance, uncompetitive elections, depressed voter turnout, underrepresentation of minorities, and even a greater risk of political violence. If there is such a thing as a scholarly consensus in political science today, it is that America's two-party system, arguably the world's strictest, is not doing our stumbling democracy any favors—and that the path out of this morass runs through more and better parties.

In fact, if there is such a thing as a consensus among Americans generally today, it is the same. Dismay with the two parties has reached new lows, with "unaffiliated" now the country's largest voting bloc. Registered partisans tend to not even like their own party as much as they simply dislike the other. A full 70 percent of Americans wish there were more. How is it, then, that in a democracy where a sizable majority prefer something else, no viable alternatives are, for the most part, ever available? The answer is both simple and arcane, located in a 1967 statute passed by Congress. Bringing multipartyism to America will require changing it.

Political competition is a function of electoral rules. Just as a duopolistic market does not come about by chance, a party system confined to only two players is a predictable consequence of rule choices. And one rule, more than any other, governs the number of nationally competitive political parties: the number of representatives elected from each legislative district.

In the United States, each congressional district sends one representative to the House. When only a single seat is up for grabs, two parties typically emerge. That is, single-member districts tend to generate predominantly two-party systems. By contrast, in a multiseat district, multiple parties have a chance at winning. More opportunities to win a seat and a lower threshold to secure one incentivizes more parties to compete. Countries like Uruguay with a modest number of seats per district (on average, 2.5) generate modest multiparty activity (there, three large parties), while others like Israel (120 seats in one nationwide district) can generate unwieldy party systems. The more seats per district, the greater the number of political parties that are likely to contest them.

This logic follows something close to a law in political science. Knowing the average number of seats per district, along with the total number of seats in a legislature, will generate a remarkably accurate prediction of the number of nationally competitive political parties in any given country.

The United States inherited its first-past-the-post electoral system from Great Britain: it was "the only game in town in 1787 and for some generations thereafter," as Robert Dahl observes. "The Framers simply left the whole matter to the states and Congress, both of which supported the only system they knew." What was bequeathed as a colonial artifact is now codified in federal law. The 1967 Uniform Congressional District Act (UCDA) is the latest, and least flexible, in a line of mandates dating back to the nineteenth century requiring the use of single-member districts for the U.S. House. Over the course of the twentieth century, as most other democracies experimented with multiparty systems, federal law largely locked the U.S. party system into place.

Any realistic effort to allow for multipartyism in America at the federal level must then contend with the UCDA. While the mandate itself is simple—it is all of a single sentence—the question of what to put in its place is less so. Instead of one representative per district, should it be six, where possible? Eight? How variable might it be from one district to the next? What about states with only a single representative, or two or three? Should Congress establish general parameters, and then otherwise let each state decide? The decisions bear directly on what a new multiparty landscape would look like.

Amending the UCDA could force other policy decisions that would also influence the nature of America's party system. For example, in multimember districts, parties should win seats in rough proportion to their votes. In a six-seat district, if a party wins 50 percent of the vote, it should win three seats. If that party had won

Tudor & Lindgrensavage

49 percent of the vote, it should still probably get three seats; but some standard allocation formula would be required to say so—and certain formulas tend to favor larger parties over smaller ones. Or consider the size of the House, which also influences the number of viable parties. It, too, should probably increase, but by how much? Without expansion, Massachusetts's nine districts could be easily collapsed into three, each sending three representatives to Congress. But nothing would change for neighboring Rhode Island with its lone representative.

Of course, policymaking can only go so far in designing a multiparty system. Various features of the U.S. political system are likely to cut against the number of new national parties. The presidency, for example—an inescapably single-winner race—would almost certainly continue to be a contest between the two major parties (though as in other presidential systems, each could form electoral coalitions with minor parties). And while federal law can create *space* for more parties, parties must still be *built*—and a variety of state-level regulations, such as restrictive ballot access laws, inhibit the ability of new parties to form and contest elections. Among the most significant barriers are state laws banning fusion voting, arguably the most successful ballot mechanism in U.S. history that supported the development of minor parties.

Loosening these restrictions is a here-and-now place to start for reformers, as Drutman rightly argues. Several organizations—including ours, Protect Democracy—are litigating to overturn bans on fusion and exploring ballot measures to advance multipartyism in state legislatures. Contending with federal law may be an important long-term ambition, but in the short-term, we need not wait for Congress to start the work of building a multiparty America. Despite different timescales and levels of government, the locus of reform is the same: revisiting the rudimentary rules that quietly structure the American party system. The goal should not be to circumnavigate parties, no matter how dismal their current performance, but to build more of them.

Here again we agree with Drutman: no matter how broadly or deeply disliked, political parties are indispensable to modern democracy. They are the institutional vehicles that connect citizens across common sets of interests, mobilize them, marshal resources, mediate coalitions, cohere policy ideas, and coordinate policymaking. When incumbent parties calcify, other parties should compete to speak to the disaffected—and in most democracies, they do. "In a multi-party democracy, politicians, activists, and voters can leave a party if they are dissatisfied with it and join or even create another," write political scientists Hans Noel and Seth Masket. But "this is close to impossible in the United States."

The reason is not for lack of trying. Today, third-party bids are drawing in millions of dollars, but they will inevitably flounder. "Independents" will outnumber both Republicans and Democrats in the 2024 election, though nearly all will vote for major party candidates anyway. Primary voters are signaling displeasure with their choices on both sides, but most will fall in line by November. While a flurry of popular reforms promising to "give voters more choice," from open primaries to ranked choice voting, are proliferating across the states, none will result in more parties winning seats.

That's because, despite the consensus and energy for change, the single-member rule, more than any other, binds the United States to a two-party system. Until it changes, we're bound to its consequences, too.

SIGN ME UP!
Joel Rogers

I HOPE Drutman's smart essay is widely read and moves readers to action. In some places I dissent from his argument, and in other places I see room for improvement. Before getting to either, however, let me state my agreement with most of what Drutman has to say.

I agree that American democracy is in crisis and that changing our current party system is key to restoring its health. Having only two tribal and fully nationalized parties—each effectively uniform across branches and chambers and between national, state, and local government—is a truly terrible way to run a country as diverse and evenly divided on national identity as the United States. It promotes a win-or-die polarization that breeds instability while negating responsible government and ruining our civic health. The fact that this system is overwhelmingly funded by the rich—and shaped by a media ecosystem that is guided more by a quest for conflict and clickbait than truth—only makes it more repellant to American patriots.

I also agree that political parties are indispensable to mass democracy. Among what political scientists call civil society's "secondary associations" (as opposed to the "primary" ones of family, religion, or nation)—a vast field including professional associations, business groups, lobbying organizations, unions, advocacy organizations, cooperatives, charitable organizations, and the like—parties are the most important to democracy. That is because they are the only ones that directly involve individual citizens in what defines democracy itself: self-rule with equal respect among the rulers. Parties also prepare citizens for such rule. They develop citizens' civic muscles and habits of democratic association by inviting and enabling them to engage in all sorts of political action. And the policy platforms candidates run on give time-short and information-scarce citizens cognitive relief and political identity—a way to make sense of the world and see their values and interests potentially expressed in policy. Political parties do this for many people at once, enabling the reduction in choices needed for millions of votes to be signals rather than mere noise.

I also agree that serious reform of this party system should take parties themselves as its focus, including their enabling conditions and the rules governing their interaction. This sensible suggestion breaks with the bounds of current electoral reform discussion, which instead focuses nearly exclusively on candidates: improving the terms on which campaigns are funded (e.g., New York City's or Seattle's public subsidies), where they are chosen ("jungle" primaries, "final four"), or how voter preferences are aggregated ("ranked choice voting" or "Condorcet"). There are things that might be said on behalf of each of these reforms, though some are deeply antidemocratic. But common to all of them is a focus on individuals, not the parties and rules that define our system. If our broken system is a room, these proposals amount to changing its drapes rather than its furniture.

And, finally, I am all for Drutman's central recommendations on how to make more meaningful changes: proportional representation (PR) and, more immediately, the recovery of the plural-nomination or "fusion" option in U.S. party politics. PR would repeal the basic rule—found nowhere in our Constitution but legislated by the two major parties, which it benefits—that elections in the United States are decided by a plurality (sometimes a majority) of votes in single-member election districts, where the winner takes all (i.e., is the only representative of that district). Implementing PR would entail multimember districts, with seats competed for by more parties. Applied nationally, this system would almost certainly require an increase in the number of elected representatives in our many legislative bodies, including Congress.

But while possibilities for municipal PR abound, its near-term national prospects are roughly zero. Fusion would be a more modest change. It is the distinctive American way of giving real weight to minority electoral sentiment, allowing voters to vote their values without wasting their votes. Like PR, it would generate more parties. But unlike PR, it has a very long history of productive use in the United States and encourages bigger winning pluralities. All these things, I think, give fusion a better chance of success here than PR.

But so much for where I agree. My chief disagreement is with Drutman's claim that our party system is the root cause of our present democratic crisis. I disagree because democratic government is today challenged all over the globe—including in many multiparty systems, with proportional representation of the sort Drutman favors. As an ideal of order, democracy has no rivals in global public opinion, but citizen confidence in it as a form of government has reached record lows, while dissatisfaction with their own governments record highs. We need a less U.S.-centric view of democracy's current troubles.

My own view includes these elements, common to virtually all the world's democracies.

First, there is the detritus of our half-century, transnational, elite-led experiment with neoliberalism. Governments around the world have retreated from protecting their citizens from corporate predation and given more authority to less regulated markets. The result has done tremendous damage to all sorts of enablers of collective action and people's confidence in government.

Second, there has been an independent crisis of state competence and legitimacy. Ever-growing interdependence and complexity (and growing recognition of both) has increased demand for a variety of essential new public goods (non-excludable and non-rival), including the ability to provide customized—and certainly non-actuarial—social supports. The former excites free-riders and those resenting contribution; the latter are nearly exactly the thing most public bureaucracies are not set up to do, and broadly incapable of doing within prevailing ideas of rule of law.

Third, we have seen the erosion of the public sphere and mutual trust. Occasioned in part by the two phenomena just noted, this trend has been further fueled by the tech-enabled fragmentation of media audiences, the collapse of local print media, the rise of massively divisive social media, and the simultaneous decline of all sorts of collective organizations: unions, churches, encompassing community organizations, sports clubs, and so on. The "public" is now a largely fugitive character.

The result is that people are more isolated from and fearful of others and understandably less confident of or inclined to positive collective action, which is what democracy is about. In this world, democracy's doldrums are not puzzling.

Of course, in recent years, neoliberalism's choking grip has loosened. New knowledge and tech offer humanity a pretty clear choice. They can be used to address Keynes's "permanent problem" of living "wisely and agreeably and well" with each other and nature from a more pacific urbanized world of egalitarian democratic abundance. Alternatively, we can allow them to be used to produce unprecedented inequality, more efficient domination, unending war, and biosphere destruction. It would be nice to organize more political communities competing for public power with alternative suggestions for its use—that is, more political parties—to guide us in that choice. But that's what our present party system makes nearly impossible.

I conclude with three bits of advice to those who want to improve that system by recovering the fusion option within it. First, we need ballot-line (or "disaggregated") fusion. It's not enough to cluster multiple fusing parties on one ballot line; their lines must first be separated, before votes cast on them are combined. Second, the benefits of this approach can be easily defeated by excessive requirements on qualifying for and then maintaining ballot status, so both of these processes must be watched. And third, fusion has no friends with power. Beneficiaries of the two-party duopoly will resist, as will federal courts still bound by the pathetically regressive 1997 opinion in *Timmons*, where the Supreme Court affirmed its reverential loyalty both to the two-party system and present occupants of that duopoly. That basically leaves only state courts and especially referenda—available in twenty-six states and hundreds of cities.

But that's certainly enough to get started, so let's get to it!

THE WRONG DIRECTION
Ian Shapiro

DRUTMAN CAN'T POSSIBLY be right that the two-party system is "the whole ballgame." The hyperpartisanship and dysfunctional politics that concerns him is happening not just in countries with two-party systems like Britain and the United States, but also in countries with multiparty systems like France and Germany and in countries dominated by a single party like South Africa. Other factors are obviously at work.

The most important is the disappearance of inclusive economic growth. This trend started at the end of the 1970s but accelerated after communism collapsed. Capital became much more mobile than labor, leaving workers more insecure as jobs disappeared offshore and, increasingly, to technology. The benefits of economic growth accrued almost exclusively to the very rich, while incomes for the bottom 90 percent either declined or were maintained only by households shifting from one to two earners or borrowing home equity—eroding middle- and working-class wealth as well.

Most people now work harder to stay in the same place. Even in a rich country like the United States, they have scant margin for error. In 2022 some 37 percent of Americans reported that they could not find $400 for an emergency without borrowing—up by 5 percent since the previous year and by 13 percent since 2013. Comparably widespread insecurity prevails in most capitalist democracies. In short, people are afraid and angry, and their futures look bleak. Many expect their children to face even worse prospects. Why wouldn't they abandon the parties that have been governing them?

Those parties have been failing them for decades. The pattern began with left-of-center parties, whose leaders found themselves back on their heels due to the apparent failure of Keynesian policies to deal with the stagflation of the 1970s and the discrediting of planned economies after 1989. They concluded that the route to power was to embrace the new supply-side orthodoxy of low taxes, low regulation, free trade, and privatization. In the United States, Democrats from Jimmy Carter to Barack Obama governed as though their job was to be better neoliberals than the Republicans. Britain's New Labour was a carbon copy. In France, Socialist Party President François Mitterrand performed a U-turn toward austerity. In Germany, a coalition of the Social Democrats and the Greens implemented the pro-business Hartz reforms. Even the African National Congress abandoned its traditional Marxism for the standard neoliberal diet on coming to power in 1994. Meanwhile, center-right parties responded by moving even further right, dragging the center-left with them. In 2007 Alan Greenspan remarked that it didn't matter which party won because the same pro-market policies would prevail either way.

All the while, the mainstream parties were sawing off the branches they were sitting on. The bipartisan commitment to largesse for the rich and austerity for the rest alienated many voters from the established parties. It animated the antisystem outrage of the Occupy Wall Street movement. But it also empowered innovative populists like Donald Trump, Nigel Farage, and Marine Le Pen, and it prompted mainstream politicians like Boris Johnson, Viktor Orbán, and Tayyip Erdoğan to morph into populists. This environment made it easy to mobilize voter support by blaming elites and immigrants for people's woes.

In multiparty systems, the result was fragmentation. Even in Germany, often touted as the model multiparty system, the share of the two largest parties declined from 78 percent of the vote in 1994 to less than 50 percent in 2021, so that for the first time in the country's history it took three ideologically incompatible parties to form a government. The dysfunctional result is so unpopular that in June this year they were hammered by the populist far right in elections for the European Parliament. Ditto for France, where Emmanuel Macron's Renaissance party achieved less than half the vote of Le Pen's National Rally—forcing him into early national elections in July, when Le Pen's party gained 54 seats in the National Assembly over the 89 it already had. Macron now has the unenviable task of trying to hold together a right-of-center governing coalition that faces a larger alliance of left parties that agree on little besides their antipathy for the right.

Voter fear and rage plays out differently in two-party systems, mostly in demands for more internal party democracy. In the United

States, it shows up in the toxic mix of safe seats and low-turnout primaries dominated by activists on the extremes. This phenomenon pulls the parties apart. Most Senate seats and more than 90 percent of House seats are no longer competitive in general elections. The problem is worse on the GOP side because it has more safe seats. As well as being unable to compromise on legislation with Democrats, Republicans can't even agree among themselves; those in safe seats veto what those in competitive seats support and vice versa. This reduces them to passing symbolic bills that never become law, pursuing investigations and impeachments, and fighting over their own leaders. Meanwhile, in the UK, the phenomenon has often played out by empowering party members—the British equivalent of primary voters—to choose unrepresentative party leaders. Threats of "entryism," the British equivalent of a primary challenge, have similar effects on candidate selection.

But isn't pulling the parties apart a good thing? It would be if the parties were internally strong. The problem today is that they are so weak that leaders can't line up support for legislative agendas that they know would appeal to most voters.

Most obviously needed are public investments in the real economy and policies that create private-sector incentives to do the same. Instead, we get populists who exploit voter anxiety by promoting xenophobia and bread-and-circuses economics: crumbs for people at the bottom while protecting those at the top. Trump's recent proposal to abolish federal taxes on tips for service workers, made the same week that he promised additional corporate tax cuts, is a case in point.

Drutman's proposal—fusion voting—pushes in the wrong direction. As with France's two-round voting system or instant runoff systems, fusion voting would keep small parties alive in hopes of influencing the larger parties. Larger parties might move to the electoral middle as a result, but that is far from obvious. It could equally pull them toward ideological extremes, as Le Pen's National Rally has done in France. Or small parties might extract clientelist benefits, as when farmers' parties demand subsidies and tariffs on food imports in exchange for their support. What would the price be for endorsement on a Tea Party line?

It would be better to attack the problem through redistricting to reduce the number of safe seats in Congress. Doing so would weaken the power of unrepresentative primary voters, because catering to them means losing in the general election. It would also weaken the hold that someone like Trump can have over congressional Republicans by threatening to support primary challenges to those who thwart him.

The good news is that more than a third of the states have already relocated redistricting from state legislatures to independent or bipartisan commissions, reflecting growing appreciation of the problem. The goal should be to create districts that are competitive between the parties, restoring incentives for candidates to head for the electoral middle. This requires large diverse districts that include urban, rural, and suburban voters and look more or less like one another. The United States already has large districts, but they stand in dire need of this kind of diversification.

Given the tendency of primaries to empower extremes, another good reform would be to let congressional party leaders override primaries and pick candidates if turnout falls below some threshold, say 70 percent of the previous general election's turnout. The same rule could apply at the presidential level, making the U.S. system more like it was before 1824, when a congressional caucus chose a party's presidential candidate. It is vital that the authority to select candidates devolve to congressional party leaders, not the infamous party bosses in smoke-filled rooms who ruled before the heyday of primaries—and who provided the impetus for decentralizing reforms in the first place.

THE LABOR OF POLITICS
Bob Master

DRUTMAN MAKES an important and provocative contribution to a debate that American trade union progressives have long wrestled with: How should unions engage in politics? Should we work solely to advance the short-term interests of dues-paying members, or are the fortunes of union members best served when the working class as a whole rises? The answer matters for labor's partisan posture. Should we be all in on the Democratic Party or seek some form of political independence? Drutman's work helps answer these questions.

The early American Federation of Labor (AFL), under the leadership of Samuel Gompers, practiced what became known as political "voluntarism"—trying to legislate conditions that smoothed the way for affiliates to negotiate "voluntary" collective bargaining agreements with employers. The federation therefore prioritized what sociologist Robin Archer has called "negative goals"—basically, preventing the state from intervening against workers in bargaining disputes, commonly via injunctions and all too often, armed force.

These mostly craft unions believed that class-wide standards on wages, hours, and working conditions (except for women and children) would dilute the appeal of unionization. Improvements like old age pensions or health insurance should be won at the bargaining table, they argued, not in the legislature. And the AFL studiously avoided partisan alignment. In 1895 it enacted a resolution declaring that "party politics whether democratic, republican, socialistic, prohibition, or any other, should have no place in the convention of the A. F. of L."

Radicals and labor militants of various stripes contested this approach, believing that labor needed independent political power. In the early 1890s, military interventions against steel strikers at Homestead and against Eugene Debs and the American Railway Union at Pullman confirmed that labor needed new levers to bend government to its needs. The Populist Party tried to bring together workers and small farmers later in that decade, and a number of Farmer-Labor parties were created at the state level in the years after World War I.

Ultimately, during the great crisis of the 1930s, a clear alternative to Gompersian voluntarism took shape within the rising industrial union movement: the social democratic or Congress of Industrial Organizations (CIO) orientation to politics. The industrial unions recognized that legislating minimum standards on wages and hours, as well as old age protection and unemployment, would make it harder for any employer to take the low road and sweat labor. Out of this second tradition emerged labor's advocacy for the signature policies of the New Deal and the Great Society: Social Security, unemployment insurance, minimum wage and maximum hours laws, occupational safety and health standards, and ultimately, civil and voting rights for Black Americans.

In February 1936, the United Mine Workers journal explained the new approach:

> Political action will . . . be increasingly necessary for two reasons: first to safeguard the fundamental principles and rights of industrial democracy; and second, in order to secure legislative and perhaps constitutional sanctions for its economic program.

The CIO won major shopfloor as well as political and legislative victories during the Depression years, and the labor movement began to see the Democrats as a labor party in spirit if not in name. Still, the impulse to independent politics didn't vanish entirely. In 1936 the Clothing Workers and Ladies Garment Workers unions joined forces to found the American Labor Party (ALP) in New York, primarily to capture the votes of socialist-oriented immigrants who might not otherwise vote for major party nominees. That year, Roosevelt garnered almost 325,000 votes on the ALP line in the state. The next year, the ALP delivered nearly half a million votes—almost 22 percent of the total—to Republican-ALP Mayoral candidate, Fiorello La Guardia.

But by the end of World War II, labor was well integrated into the New Deal state and fully ensconced in the Democratic Party. Labor's stature as the predominant "interest group" in the Democratic Party was symbolized by the quadrennial kickoff event of every Democratic presidential campaign through 1964, a massive rally in Detroit's Cadillac Square.

In retrospect, however, labor's power was never as secure as its leadership hoped. In 1947 an alliance of anti-union business interests (largely in the GOP) and anti-union segregationists (entirely in the Democratic Party) united to pass the Taft-Hartley Act, which the labor movement denounced as "slave-labor legislation." The CIO's broad social democratic ambitions were frozen. Union members enjoyed growing economic prosperity and retirement security, but these arrived via a collectively bargained "private welfare state." Organized labor was able to win few class-wide victories. The one major exception—the creation of Medicare—only proved the general rule. Labor's forward march was not halted, but it had slowed.

By the mid-1970s, labor's subordinate role within the Democratic Party was painfully apparent. Carter abandoned labor law reform and deregulated the trucking and airline industries, with devastating consequences for workers and their unions. Reagan crushed the PATCO workers as a signal that it was open season on unions. Clinton administered the *coup de grâce* of NAFTA, promoted China's admission to the WTO, and deregulated finance for good measure. Obama followed the advice of his neoliberal Treasury team, failing to jail a single banker after the financial fraud of 2008, and pushed for passage of a Pacific region version of NAFTA right through his final days in office.

All in all, this was evidence of what former UAW President Doug Fraser had called "a one-sided class war" after the scuttling of labor law reform back in 1978. In the last decades of the twentieth century, no sober observer of American politics could argue that the Democratic Party was a "labor party," even in spirit. In this new context, the long-simmering question of labor's political independence inevitably regained traction.

Which brings us back to Drutman and the crucial role of parties as vehicles for political change. New York state was not immune to global neoliberal trends, and by 1998 policymaking in Albany mimicked that of Washington: business-dominated and disdainful of more generous social provision, with just an occasional minor concession to organized labor. But New York's unique fusion laws made possible the creation of a non-spoiler independent political organization, and a handful of progressive-minded labor and community leaders decided to launch a new effort in 1998. The New York Working Families Party (WFP) was born.

Our aim was to build a community-labor coalition party with the capacity to broadcast a pro–working-class political agenda and the power to hold Democrats accountable to it. That it turned out somewhat better than expected would be an understatement. The WFP anchored the transformation of state politics and governance over the next twenty-five years. The capacity to identify and train candidates, develop campaign staff, mount issue campaigns (like raising the minimum wage or increasing taxes on the wealthy), unite with Democrats to defeat reactionaries in general elections, maintain the capacity to challenge antilabor Democrats in primaries, build relationships of mutual respect with legislative leadership, raise money, and work the political press—it all added up to organization and power.

The party was able to do all of this for one reason alone: the rules in New York state kept us out of the wasted vote or spoiler boxes, allowing a multiracial, working-class, and highly competent political party to emerge and thrive on a *year-round* basis. Mistakes were made along the way, but having a permanent party organization allows the time and space for course correction.

Drutman's advocacy for the centrality of parties is entirely correct. Politics is hard, and fusion is just one of the many reforms we need. But it solves one fundamental problem for unions and other organized groups of citizens: you can be both independent *and* relevant. It's easy to be independent and *irrelevant*, but if you're reading this, that's not your bag. You need fusion voting.

BUILDING A UNITED FRONT
Maurice Mitchell & Doran Schrantz

DRUTMAN MAKES a persuasive and important case about both the need and the strategy for moving beyond a sclerotic two-party system. His core recommendation—reviving fusion voting to empower more parties—would simultaneously protect and invigorate American democracy. We must embrace politics by creating new vehicles for individuals to participate in collective political expression while also incentivizing electoral and governing coalitions.

History teaches us that defeating authoritarian movements requires an expansive, potent "united front" that might not agree on much besides their preference for living in a pluralist democracy. Drutman lays out how fusion voting could empower disaffected conservative and independent voters who are dismayed by Trump and Trumpism, but are not at all at home in the Democratic Party, to create a robust new political identity. One can only devoutly hope they do so. Does it make us uncomfortable, given our differences with such people on too many topics to mention? Of course.

But a united front implies a wide range of forces, and if you're not uncomfortable, your movement probably is not that wide and definitely won't be powerful.

Fusion could also do the same for the left. This year, some voters who are discouraged or angered by the Democrats' stance on Israel and Palestine will undoubtedly be tempted by quixotic minor-party presidential campaigns or, even more likely, opt out of the election altogether. In this context, imagine what a fusion-legal system would mean in, say, Pennsylvania or Michigan.

The Working Families Party is publicly 100 percent pro-ceasefire and is working hard to pressure the Biden administration and Congress to change course. Many progressive organizations actively engaged in "uncommitted" campaigns that carried a similar "pro-ceasefire, anti–unconditional aid" during the Democratic presidential primary, producing north of 10 percent of the vote in Minnesota, Michigan, and New York. These campaigns gave voters a way to actively participate in a party endorsement process, making them much more likely to keep participating through the November election.

Progressive groups and many "uncommitted" voters understand the danger of a Trump restoration. In a fusion-legal electoral regime, a pragmatic and principled minor party could organize a very powerful message: "The Democrats have been wrong on Gaza, and if you share that view, then vote for the Democratic nominee on a pro-ceasefire line and send a powerful message. It keeps Trump out of power, but also says to the Democrats, 'You must change course.'" There is little question in our minds that such a party would get a solid chunk of votes, but instead of *spoiling* the election, it would help *save* it. Instead of these voters opting out, they can opt in: fusion would give them a powerful, proactive, and electoral means of expression.

Ultimately, we know that the best long-term bulwark against authoritarianism is to increase voter agency and democratic participation. Changing the rules of our electoral system—including but by no means limited to party-centric reforms like fusion—is thus of utmost importance. In Minnesota, the We Choose Us coalition won an astounding set of reforms to democratic practice in 2023, including restoring the right to vote for those who have a felony conviction, automatic voter registration, and pre-registration for sixteen and seventeen year olds.

These changes clear the way for more voters to participate, but voting itself does not transform an individual into a political actor who has the experience of agency. That requires a means of collective expression—organizations and parties that bundle shared interests into political power. We Choose Us, like the WFP, is a broad-based, community-labor coalition. In a sense, it bundles "people's organizations" into a quasi-party that can advance a shared interest in voting rights and multiracial democracy, and as such it validates Drutman's point that "partisanship" is not the source of America's broken politics. The problem is that there are only *two* parties, limiting the political expression of all of their "parts," increasing cynicism and dissatisfaction within the voting public, and creating perverse incentives in the policy-making process.

Reformers who decry "polarization" are working to take the politics out of politics. This is a fool's errand. Individuals don't engage in political participation in an interest-free vacuum; the truth—as every organizer knows—is that people naturally band together under common interests and build vehicles to advance them. That's the essence of civil society. And when voters don't see themselves or their interests reflected in those vehicles, they are less likely to vote at all. If we want more people to participate—and to participate in a way that genuinely captures and reflects their values—then we need more vehicles.

But fusion does more than just increase the participation of individual voters. It also strengthens the political, small "d" democratic landscape, which we believe is necessary for democratic resilience moving forward. Fusion can strengthen and incentivize the power of people-centered organizations that build new, minor parties. Former ACORN leader Bertha Lewis and former Citizen Action of New York director Karen Scharff have both argued that being part of a political party opened doorways and opportunities to statewide power far beyond the local bases and power centers of their organizations. It also incentivizes bargaining and coalition between major and minor parties, which means those same community and labor organizations have more ability to negotiate policy victories.

This dynamic has proven especially valuable for increasing Black and brown political power. The community groups that helped build WFP in New York and Connecticut had primarily Black and brown membership bases. In states without fusion, the influence of these groups is largely limited to the majority-minority Congressional and legislative districts of their members. But by having a statewide ballot line, they were able to build cross-region multiracial coalitions and project power far beyond their traditional geographic strongholds. In a sense, fusion provides a powerful complement to voting rights laws: it builds power for Black Americans that amplifies the Black representation gains inherent in the (now weakened) Voting Rights Act. This goes for Native, Chicano, Latino power in the Southwest, and Asian communities on the West Coast and beyond.

One piece of the puzzle that Drutman doesn't mention but surely must understand is how much the major parties will oppose the relegalization of fusion voting. These institutions, which have become increasingly hollowed out of robust local participation of grassroots activists, are perfectly happy with the two-party system. And they *detest* the way that fusion parties—on the left and the right, and perhaps sooner than later in the center—can make demands on them.

In both Connecticut and New York, Republicans and Democrats have tried repeatedly over the decades to do away with fusion. Most famously, WFP battled for years with Andrew Cuomo. WFP was the nerve center for a broad network of organizations who took him on directly, ending the Republican majority he orchestrated in the Senate. Cuomo struck back hard, threatening union affiliates and even changing ballot access rules to destroy the state's minor parties. He failed, but the fact that he tried so aggressively to functionally ban fusion is a testament to the power conferred by the ballot line.

Of course, no single reform is a silver bullet. There is an enormous amount of coalition building underway in the forty-eight non-fusion states that is just as good and important as that in the two fusion states, and the work to legalize fusion is going to take some time. But electoral politics and functional governing coalitions are essential to achieving our ends. Power never concedes anything without a demand, and nothing turns demands into progress like a party.

ESCAPING THE DOOM LOOP

Lee Drutman

THESE RESPONSES HIGHLIGHT the severity of the democratic challenges we face and the necessity of debate in assessing paths forward. Three key themes emerge.

First, most respondents agree that political organizations, particularly political parties, are essential vehicles for democratic engagement and representation. Modern democracy *is* party democracy. And because fusion is a party-centric reform, it has unique power.

Second, several question whether fusion voting on its own would make enough of a difference given the scale of the problems, and whether other approaches might be more powerful. No doubt, *many* changes would make for a healthier democracy and improve our political culture. But because parties are the core institutions of modern representative democracy, everything else runs through the party system.

Third, a few highlight obstacles to reviving fusion in states where it has been outlawed. After all, fusion challenges the dominance of the two major parties; their leaders have objected—and will object—to its expansion. Is there really a feasible way around these obstacles? I believe there is.

Start with the role of political organization and political parties.

Factors beyond parties have certainly contributed to our current predicament. Ian Shapiro argues that "the disappearance of inclusive economic growth" has wreaked political havoc. Deepak Bhargava and Arianna Jiménez likewise point to "the rise of grotesque economic inequality," while Joel Rogers blames neoliberalism and a collapse of the public sector. But Rogers also rightly notes that without vibrant, multiparty competition for public power, alternative visions for a more inclusive economic system are more easily pushed to the margins. Indeed, scholars have found consistent evidence that democracies with institutionalized multiparty systems have lower levels of economic inequality and higher levels of economic redistribution—consistent with Rogers's argument.

It is true that we see turmoil across different party systems. But among rich democracies, the United States stands out in its high inequality, low public investment, and most significantly, the rise of a major political party that has turned hostile to the basic foundations of liberal democracy. Despite America's uniquely resilient post-pandemic economy, our politics are anything but. Our major parties limp forward by default. Despite their failures, they persist because they have a monopoly on opposition to each other.

Shapiro's preferred remedy is to increase electoral competition through independent redistricting commissions—a widely proposed solution. But geographic partisan sorting—the fact that Democrats dominate in cities and dense suburbs, while Republicans dominate in sparse suburbs, exurbs, and small towns—poses an extreme problem for this approach. It's hard to draw evenly competitive districts without making districts that stretch beyond meaningful coherence. Even in states that have used such commissions, the vast majority of districts—more than 80 percent—are still safe for one party.

Daniel Schlozman and Sam Rosenfeld also want stronger parties. I agree wholeheartedly with their assessment that today's "hollow parties" also make for a very hollow version of democracy. But their preferred approach, laid out even more fully in their new book by that name, is a bullhorn cry to party leaders and donors: reinvest in the lost values of grounded and rooted political parties, with real presences in real places.

But parties invest in local organizing only if doing so pays off in wins. In their book, Schlozman and Rosenfeld sing the praises of the Nevada Democratic Party and the impressive organized machine that Harry Reid built around it, in which Las Vegas unions have real on-the-ground power. But what goes on in Nevada might well stay there. Most states, like most congressional districts, are so safe for one party that no amount of on-the-ground organizing could make a difference, at least in the foreseeable future.

If we change the electoral rules, however, we change how votes matter, even in the short term. Reforms like fusion and proportional representation can encourage party organizing for a simple reason: the payoff changes when more voters matter. Like Bhargava and Jiménez, I think our democracy would benefit from more civic organizing. But mobilizing and motivating citizens to join and participate in civil society groups is harder when they don't see themselves represented in the political system. It's also hard when too many people don't feel that participation matters, often because existing incumbents in safe districts can safely ignore them.

Like Schlozman and Rosenfeld, I agree we should do more than just revive fusion voting. Yes, "fusion does nothing about presidentialism, never mind the Senate and the Supreme Court"—the sort of built-in structural elements that Bhargava and Jiménez also identify. But absent an unlikely—and at this moment at least, dangerous—constitutional convention, I am not sure what would address these problems. And contrary to Schlozman and Rosenfeld's outdated assertion that "multipartyism and presidentialism are a bad mix," two decades of scholarship has shown that it works just fine. The canonical paper on this finding was published three decades ago by Scott Mainwaring. Last year, Mainwaring and I wrote an updated paper, arguing that whatever risks of multiparty presidentialism might exist—and they are fewer than this outdated conventional wisdom claims—pale in comparison to the risks of polarized two-party presidentialism.

Danielle Allen argues that the "Alaska-style" electoral system is our best bet: a two-round, top-four system with ranked choice voting. For states like Alaska—with a strong independent political culture and a long history of bipartisan governing coalitions in the state legislature—this system may be a good fit. (We will see, though: Alaskans may vote to repeal it this year.) But the open primaries double down on many of the pathologies of our current situation—above all, the fact that without partisan gatekeepers, money, name recognition, and attention-grabbing skills are the most important things in politics. In

2022 the Alaska system mostly helped incumbents win. That is no surprise: incumbents are usually the ones with the most fundraising power, name recognition, and attention-grabbing capabilities.

Ranked choice voting does give voters more precise opportunities to express their preferences, and I used to think it was a very good idea. But after seeing study after study showing fewer benefits than promised and multiple studies showing significant voter confusion (particularly among lower-income, predominantly Black and brown communities), I have cooled to the idea and see more limited uses for it. Like Rogers, I worry that open primaries and ranked choice voting put too much "focus on individuals, not the parties and rules that define our system. If our broken system is a room, these proposals amount to changing its drapes rather than its furniture." I agree with Tabatha Abu El-Haj about the central importance of political parties: fusion is "a good idea because it is a party-centric reform with real potential to leverage meaningful democratic returns."

Allen is also surprisingly dismissive of the Working Families Party's presence in New York, noting the small share it claims of registered voters. Her numbers are right, but they miss the point: the party focuses on *members and supporters*, not *registrants*. (In 2020, almost 400,000 people voted for Joe Biden under the WFP label in New York.) Bob Master, a founder of New York's WFP, offers a different, insider's take. His capsule history shows how New York's fusion laws allowed the party to organize a distinct constituency, develop candidates and staff, and mount issue campaigns. A minor party can play a constructive and productive role in politics, if the rules allow it. Indeed, as Bhargava and Jiménez astutely argue, one of the strongest cases for fusion voting is how it can work synergistically with community and labor organizing. A place on the ballot is real power, and real power attracts organizers.

Maurice Mitchell, the current national director of the WFP, and Doran Schrantz importantly connect the power of more organized parties to increased democratic participation and agency. The logic is simple but profound. Parties are the natural organizing forces in politics; they are our most central "vehicles" for collective action. But when there are only two such vehicles, a lot of people feel left out—and many people disconnect from voting altogether. Fusion creates more lanes, so more vehicles can get on the political road (without the current problems that minor parties now have as potential spoilers). Under an Alaska-style system, candidates may come and go, building a list and then taking it with them. But under fusion, parties make real investments in long-term representation, as only organized political parties can and the WFP unequivocally has done.

The most ambitious critique, from Joshua Lerner, is that an elections-centered view of democracy falls far short of "genuine democracy." In our era of frustration with traditional parties and political intermediaries, I understand the appeal of other democratic forms like sortition, citizens' assemblies, and participatory budgeting. But large-scale modern democracy—with its scale, scope, complexities, and demands—requires intermediation and structure, lest it devolve into chaos. Political parties have made modern representative democracy possible by structuring and organizing alternatives in a way that does not require people to have leisure-class status to participate. Some more participatory reforms may work well at a hyperlocal level, but at a national level they ignore the hard realities of power, agenda-setting, and legitimacy.

Of course, any reform that challenges existing power structures faces significant obstacles. As several respondents note, leaders of the established parties are not likely to warm to reforms that threaten their dominance. But among potential reforms, fusion voting has one unique advantage: it offers a state-by-state litigation pathway, because many states have robust constitutions with expansive protections for freedom of association. As Abu El-Haj argues, "the prospects for reviving fusion politics are far more promising than many of the alternatives currently under consideration."

Finally, there is the question of what our ultimate goal should be. A distinct advantage of fusion voting over other reforms is that it builds toward multiparty proportional representation. As Grant Tudor and Cerin Lindgrensavage note, along with Rogers, proportional representation is the most powerful, transformative way to build a more representative, less zero-sum democracy.

The transformative nature of such reform is the appeal as well as the challenge. Fusion voting is a powerful step because it creates space for actual new parties to organize and influence elections. It thus directs reform energy towards more and better parties, as opposed to more and better candidates. New parties can further build the infrastructure and demand for full multiparty proportional representation.

There are obviously many other challenges to American democracy (and all democracies) right now, including economic inequality, the devastating impacts of climate change, rapid technological change, and more. These are hard times, with hard problems, and it is possible that modern representative party democracy simply cannot meet them. But I strongly believe it can, as long as we set the system up for success. That means enabling a party system that can represent the diversity and pluralism of the country and forge fluid coalitions so we don't get stuck fighting the same old zero-sum battles. We need to escape the two-party doom loop. And fusion is the first, and most powerful, step in that direction. ◆

Looking out past the Butterfield Trail Golf Club in El Paso, Texas. Image: Honora Spicer

POST COLONIALISM

Honora Spicer

"A WALL will be erected along the frontier," wrote a journalist along the U.S.-Mexico border. "Posting large bodies of men ... might serve the double purpose of keeping the Indians in check and protecting the mail." It was 1858, and he was riding west through Texas with a mule-pulled coach of Butterfield's Overland Mail Company. The "wall" he envisioned was a chain of fort-like postal stations, transporting mail but also facilitating the transit of settlers and curtailing Indigenous and Mexicano movement. The legacy of that project is made plain on the landscape today.

While volunteering in El Paso at an immigration detention center adjacent to the air mail facility, I noticed how crucial the post was to the administration of the center. The address required for asylum claims, the letters sent to lawyers from inside the detention center, the money orders drawn at the post office to pay bail bonds—all relied on the mail. Curious to follow the connections, earlier this year I traveled part of the historic mail route with a friend who directs migrant shelters in the region.

Driving between El Paso and Fort Davis, we pass pecan groves and cotton fields in the Lower Valley of the Rio Grande. We fill gas in Fabens and turn southbound on a road undulating through washes near Fort Quitman, a historic post stop. Arroyos are pinned with barbed wire, and we cross tracks of off-roaders, flanked by craggy rims in the wide valley. Our cell signal fades as we pass sparse RV clusters and a yellow dividing line pinched into the distance by an unseen inset river.

Outside a closed ranch gate, we pause by a flood gauge. The first auto tourists of the Texas mail had photographed the dilapidated adobe of Fort Quitman in the 1930s. In the wash beside us, the sand is smoothed by chain-pulled tires dragged by Border Patrol trucks to facilitate footprint surveillance. A Border Patrol horse trailer speeds by, and three sets of beady equine eyes stare back. When we return to the highway and cross the Border Patrol checkpoint, my friend receives WhatsApp audio messages: requests from two women for shelter in Juárez, dogs barking in the background. It would be cold that night, and so many people still needed a place to sleep.

The postal service was the largest federal presence on the Western frontier in the decades after the U.S. invasion of Mexico in 1848. Many assume the post system is simply a mechanism for delivering mail, but that effort both requires and justifies a host of other behaviors. In 1850s West Texas, proslavery politicians wanted to secure a southern transcontinental route by constructing militarized post roads and postal stations. Their federally subsidized construction limited Indigenous access to water sites and led to bids for military protection, while contractors imported guns to arm mercenary-like mail coaches.

Spicer

The post was a conduit of capital generated by extractive industries like mining and ranching, and it helped administer land offices that validated private claims to Indigenous land. The infrastructure and relationships fixed by the mail facilitated railroad construction decades later.

Today former employees, descendants of mail carriers, and mail enthusiasts often travel along the historic routes, which now cross fortified private ranches. In 1994, one Texas journalist traced the route that delivered Euro-American settlers to west Texas, to "repeat, if possible, some of the quotidian jolts, jars, hungers, and thirsts . . . which those nineteenth-century passengers endured." That same year, Operation Gatekeeper initiated a new phase of border militarization through a lethal policy forcing migrants into these remote desert regions.

In 2023, an act of Congress designated the Butterfield Overland National Historic Trail, a 3,292-mile route running from the Mississippi River to San Francisco through the southernmost states, one of twenty-one National Historic Trails. Working toward plans for building interpretive sites and roadside signs by 2026, staff from the Santa Fe–based National Trails Office are conducting public meetings along the route. They came through El Paso shortly after I returned from the road trip to Fort Davis in January 2024, and I decided to attend.

To get to the meeting, I take the on-ramp to the Border Highway at the railway bridge at Hart's Mill, an early army post and flour contract site. The dam below the highway diverts water from the Rio Grande into the American Canal. Beyond a red stoplight lies the rocky skirt of Sierra del Cristo Rey, where migrants cross trestles from Juárez. The privately funded border wall at the American Eagle Brick Company is already rusted, posts thorning the slope succumbing to cliff.

I turn onto the freight-laden interstate, elevated on pillars. A WELLS FARGO sign, marking the corporation that would purchase Butterfield's Overland Mail at the start of the Civil War, glows yellow from an office building in downtown El Paso. The Border Highway follows the wall and is already lined with Camino Real National Historic Trail signs. Construction traffic message boards euphemistically display "Watch for Unexpected Pedestrians." The next day, I read news reports that the Border Patrol detained migrants in storm drains along this stretch.

Before turning into Ascarate Park, I am passed by Border Patrol, El Paso Police, and Texas Highway Patrol vehicles. Once inside the Pavilion, I sit down with fifteen attendees in front of a PowerPoint presentation, sheltering from the dust storm that had occluded the nearby oil refinery and infilled lake.

The goal of a historic trail, the staff begin, is to highlight "events along a path that shaped us as a nation." Having come from a public meeting in Fort Davis dominated by private landowners wary of Historic Trail tourists on their land, the Parks staff emphasize their role in administering historical interpretation, not in managing any land. Here in El Paso, the meeting draws a less hostile crowd: representatives of community foundations, park rangers from local National Park Service sites, members of nearby trail associations with intersecting routes. The Park Service historian attests to the

Overland Mail's legacy as a "huge logistical undertaking" akin to early space exploration, prompting a significant infusion of cash to settlers through postal contracts and an "unprecedented extension of federal power." The triumphalist view inherent in the premise of this Historic Trail limits whose story can be told here.

Despite the Butterfield journalist's prophecy, the colonial projects of the post did not have inevitable outcomes and were contested at every stage. Apache mule raids on postal stations led to continuous postal property losses and the termination of postal contracts in 1861. Regular cross-continental mail service would not run through West Texas again until mail by rail in 1881, when the federal government was perpetrating Apache and Comanche displacement as a matter of official policy. While the period of Indigenous sovereignty in this region lasted far longer than the fleeting years during which the Butterfield route occupied a contested corridor (1858 to 1861), plans to monumentalize the historic route focus only one moment and direction of movement. Postal projects were part of a trajectory of accreting colonial uses of space, but that project remains incomplete.

The Historic Trails team share their contact information with us, eager for partnerships and to ensure that there is something for people to "see" along the route. The National Park Service is now tasked with making the historic post visible to tourists, even while state power to detain migrants, contingent on this postal history, is hidden in plain sight.

At the end of the road trip, I meet a local historian at the Butterfield Trail Golf Club, near a Texas Historical Commission marker for the Overland Mail at the club entrance. He walks me out past the westernmost holes and points to the rutted swale supposed to have been Butterfield's route. Ideally oriented toward the slope of the mountains into the Pass of the North, wind-swept sand ruts catch the lowering sun. Beyond the golf course perimeter, dimly visible, lie an airport runway and, along the historic postal route, the ICE detention center.

THE DREAM OF A RESPONSIBLE CONSERVATIVE
David Austin Walsh

J. D. VANCE'S SELECTION as Donald Trump's running mate has unnerved many Democrats. He is closely tied to the architects of Project 2025, the Heritage Foundation plan to purge large swathes of the civil service. He is friendly with Tucker Carlson, Elon Musk, and Alex Jones, and he warns darkly about falling birthrates and rising immigration. All of this strikes many as remarkable given that Vance began his political career as the darling of the liberal establishment with his 2016 book *Hillbilly Elegy*, widely praised as offering the definitive explanation of the appeal of Donald Trump to the white working class. In reality, Vance was a prominent Never Trumper in 2016, telling his former roommate that Donald Trump was "America's Hitler" and publicly declaring he would vote for a third party.

Vance's political transformation—if it is indeed even much of a transformation at all—from liberal darling to reactionary proto-fascist is easy to dismiss as simply a case of unchecked political ambition and thirst for power. The bigger story is what the fact that liberals' favorite conservative in 2016 has now aligned himself with the hard right tells us about the deeper pathologies of U.S. politics—above all, the liberal dream of finding a "responsible conservative" to spar with that would render American democracy stable and safe from partisan extremes.

Like most political categories, the term's meaning has changed over time, but in general a "responsible conservative," since the 1950s, is a right-winger who liberals consider a legitimate part of the American political order. In this sense, responsible conservatism is fundamentally an invention of the liberal political imagination. A "responsible conservative" is neither a fascist nor a reactionary, but someone who offers thoughtful critiques of the excesses of American liberalism and *especially* of the left.

The category is fluid, reflecting changing liberal conceptions about formally acceptable politics. In the 1950s, liberals saw William F. Buckley Jr. as a dangerous reactionary; by 1970, despite having more or less the same substantive political commitments, he was thought of as a responsible conservative by a liberal establishment terrified by the challenge of the New Left. Ronald Reagan, tarred as a dangerous extremist in the 1960s, was feted as a responsible conservative in the 1980s by the very same intellectuals who had condemned Buckley in the '50s, most of whom had become neo-conservatives in the meantime.

But unlike the elite and out-of-touch liberal establishment, "responsible conservatives," even when they were the products of the Yale Club, understood some deeper truths about American politics.

There is nothing more responsible, after all, than consistently winning elections.

IN THE NINETEENTH and early twentieth centuries, the phrase "responsible conservative" was practically a tautology. To be temperamentally conservative just was to be sober, responsible, and bourgeois. One Florida bank advertised in 1918 that it was a "responsible, conservative, and progressive" institution—meaning, presumably, that it was a practical and risk-averse organization while still paying close attention to the dynamics of the marketplace.

But as a distinct political category, the type only began to emerge in the 1930s to distinguish between conservatives and fascists. The *New York Herald Tribune* referred to Paul von Hindenburg and his supporters as "sober and responsible conservative elements" in July 1930 as opposed to the Nazis and their allies. By the 1940s "responsible conservative" (or more rarely "respectable conservative") was shorthand in American political discourse for "right-wing but non-Nazi." This did not imply a total wall of separation between the two—one letter writer to the *New York Times* bemoaned in 1941 that American Nazis "hide behind more respectable conservative elements"—but that the "responsible conservatives" were a legitimate element of liberal democracy and should not bear the same political stigma as Nazism.

The end of World War II and the first comprehensive defeats for the New Deal coalition in 1946 prompted a round of liberal soul-searching about the need for a responsible conservatism to temper American liberalism's reform agenda without rolling back the New Deal state. There was perhaps no greater liberal apostle of this need than Harvard historian and political pundit Arthur M. Schlesinger Jr. one of the founders of the liberal anticommunist group Americans for Democratic Action (ADA). His 1949 book *The Vital Center* was practically a manifesto for the ADA, focusing on the dangers of the "totalitarian" challenge posed by communism and the need for a robust, muscular, and militant liberalism to counter the threat, particularly overseas. Schlesinger also lamented that American conservatism lacked a Churchill—a farsighted, old-school leader savvy enough to recognize the communist threat. Instead, Schlesinger argued, American conservatives were mere "businessmen," focused on short-term gain rather than long-term social stability. While he attested that capitalism was a positive good, he did not trust the business class to be able to defend it.

Schlesinger did not seriously believe that a responsible conservatism would supplant liberal hegemony—for what made conservatism responsible was that it *accepted* the changes in American society since 1933 and merely sought to slow the pace of reform. "There is a vital difference between a conservative and a reactionary," he wrote in the *New York Times* in 1950. "A true conservative believes that the processes of change are gradual and organic. . . . but he knows well that there is a stream of history, that change does come about, and that the recognition of the necessity of change is the best way of preventing it from disrupting society." The "responsible liberal," according to Schlesinger, would rather have a strong "responsible conservative" political party win an election every now and then—an essential component of a two-party system—rather than have such a party shatter and its followers be co-opted by fascist demagoguery.

Schlesinger's policy definition of "responsible conservatism" was indistinguishable from that of contemporary liberalism. Responsible conservatives should reject tariffs and trade protectionism because the boost to domestic production would come, he wrote, "only at the expense of world economic stability." Channeling Bismarck, responsible conservatives should support social welfare, if only to "bribe the masses into loyalty" toward capitalism. Schlesinger even argued that responsible conservatives "must demand the speedy recognition of the equal rights of the Negro." He conceded that he was essentially arguing that his program for responsible conservatism was a sort of "me-tooism"—the political premise that American conservatism should be a lighter, more decentralized, and technocratically competent version of American liberalism—but he insisted that this was simply the rational response to the social, political, and technological conditions of the mid-twentieth century. Besides, there were already politicians in the Republican Party who represented the future of responsible conservatism, men like Wayne Morse, Henry Cabot Lodge, and Jacob Javits—all of whom are remembered today, if at all, as avatars of liberal Republicanism. Conservatives must follow those leaders, Schlesinger concluded, and "not [Karl] Mundt and [Richard] Nixon."

In this conceit, responsible conservatism also implied fervent support for America's global anticommunist role in the Cold War. In a 1951 resolution passed at its national convention, the ADA condemned what it called the "Taft-McCarthy alliance" between Ohio senator Robert Taft and the infamous Wisconsin demagogue Joseph McCarthy, as well as other Republican leaders who, "abandoning the role of a responsible conservatism have formed [this] alliance based on disguised isolationism and cynical demogy [sic] . . . at the cost of this country's position in the world." Still, the ADA's vision was not universal—some proponents of "responsible conservatism," like newspaperman Marquis Childs, called Taft "as near to being a responsible conservative as our political system produces" despite his opposition to NATO and the United Nations. *The Reporter*, a hawkish anticommunist liberal magazine, avowed that Nixon was the "responsible and more effective alternative to Senator McCarthy."

"RESPONSIBLE CONSERVATISM," in short, was a moving target—a category that conservatives could flit in and out of depending on the specific demands of the political moment. While McCarthy would remain universally despised by liberals as "irresponsible," men with the same substantive political commitments—but without McCarthy's crude aesthetics—could be welcomed under the cloak of respectability.

Nowhere was this more evident than in Buckley's political transformation. The *enfant terrible* of the New Right was nearly universally despised by liberals and even many responsible conservatives when he first rose to prominence in the early 1950s. Peter Viereck and McGeorge Bundy—both on Schlesinger's list of "responsible conservatives"—were unstinting in their criticism, the former saying that Buckley offered "the most sterile Old Guard brand of Republicanism, far to the right of Taft" and the latter writing that "I find the book is dishonest in its use of facts, false in its theory, and a discredit to its author." Seymour Lipset, in his contribution to the influential 1955 edited volume *The New American Right*, decries Buckley as the "McCarthy's young intellectual spokesman"—Buckley having just written a book-length defense of McCarthy—and laments that while Buckley and other rising conservative intellectuals like James Burnham preach a kind of free-market libertarianism, Buckley himself urged in *God and Man at Yale* (1951) a purge of American universities.

In his contribution to the volume, historian Richard Hofstadter did not address Buckley directly but tried to make sense of what he called the "new dissent" from the right more broadly. Borrowing the term "pseudo-conservative" from Theodor Adorno's *The Authoritarian Personality* (1950), Hofstadter used the phrase to attempt to describe and define the emerging conservative movement of the decade. "They have little in common with the temperate and compromising spirit of true conservatism in the classical sense of the word," he wrote. While it would be reductive to say that "the new pseudo-conservatism is simply the old ultra-conservatism and the old isolationism," it would not be inaccurate, although Hofstadter also took pains to emphasize that pseudo-conservatism is not "purely and simply fascist or totalitarian." But he did consider pseudo-conservatives to be radicals, as did the other contributors to the volume, including Lipset, Daniel Bell, and Nathan Glazer.

Even the revised and expanded edition of the book published in 1962—prompted by the rise of the John Birch Society—included *National Review* on the list of radical right-wing publications. Anti-Defamation League chiefs Arnold Forster and Benjamin R. Epstein labeled Buckley an "Extreme Conservative" in their 1964 book *Danger on the Right*, who served as an "ideological bridge" between the radical right and responsible conservatives.

But what a difference a mid-Atlantic accent makes! By the mid-1960s Buckley had savvily positioned himself as the "responsible conservative" with whom liberals could congenially debate the issues of the day. Even Forster and Epstein were forced to concede Buckley's "attractiveness, erudition, charm, intelligence, and wit." Despite his continued and outspoken support for McCarthy and his calls to purge the Ivy League, Buckley was friendly with leading liberal intellectuals and celebrities, including Schlesinger and TV host Steve Allen, with whom he often appeared in public debates. (To be fair, Buckley also debated James Baldwin in 1965, and Baldwin emphatically did *not* consider Buckley his friend.) Buckley's TV program *Firing Line* also did wonders for his reputation as the witty, urbane, and responsible conservative for liberals to be in dialogue with, a necessary check on liberal ambition and self-importance. This persona was made even more magnetic following the insurgent challenges of the New Left. In his 1965 book *Letter to a Conservative*, which emphasized the need for a strong conservative movement to restore "rationality to the American political dialogue," Steve Allen also warned of the rising danger from the left and that responsible conservatives were vital allies of sane liberals.

Indeed, "responsible conservative" as a political term lost much of its moxie in the 1970s and 1980s, as many liberals began their long march to the right in response to the New Left insurgency. By the end of the 1970s, most of the contributors to *The New American Right* were staunch neoconservatives. (The notable exception was Hofstadter, whose political drift was interrupted by his sudden death in 1970.) The increasing influence of the conservative movement had moved the Overton window of responsible conservatism so significantly that Barry Goldwater and Ronald Reagan, condemned in the sixties as dangerous radicals, now found a place entirely within the mainstream of American politics.

Furthermore, liberals could no longer approach conservatives with a degree of condescending detachment. Buckley had grown into something more than simply the intellectual sparring partner of the liberal establishment—he was a powerful political figure in his own right, especially given his close relationship with Reagan. And Reagan's repeated crushing political victories over the Democratic Party in the 1980s underwrote liberal anxieties. Ironically Schlesinger, of all people, wrote in 1986 that "Democrats feel that President Reagan knows a secret and that if they could only learn the secret they could be as popular as he." Schlesinger warned that Democrats should resist the temptation to go all in "for cutting back social programs, for deregulation, for abandonment of racial minorities, for dumping [the New Deal and Great Society] into the ash heap of history, and for worshipping at the shrine of the free market." Democrats, of course, did *not* follow Schlesinger's advice. Instead, Al From's Democratic Leadership Council and the Third Way ideology of the Clinton administration fully embraced

Reaganite me-tooism—in essence, becoming the "responsible liberals" in a period of conservative hegemony.

THE RISE of Trump—especially after an era where the Democratic Party was supposed to have learned the lessons of Reaganism—sparked another liberal crisis of confidence. Ever since MAGAism came on the political scene there has been a pronounced tendency among American liberals toward nostalgia for the good old days of civil and responsible discourse, a time when bipartisanship ruled the day on Capitol Hill and the far left and far right were both marginal forces. In essence, this is the same vision that the ADA had elaborated in the 1940s and 1950s—but even the ADA was not looking backward. It understood that state of affairs to be a political project that remained to be built.

The reactionary nostalgia trap of post-2016 liberalism brings us back to Vance. When he burst on the scene with *Hillbilly Elegy*—which drew critical acclaim from the liberal establishment, and quickly led to a post as a contributor at CNN—Vance was already the perfect archetype of a responsible conservative. For one, he had the right credentials—he was a military veteran, a Yale Law School grad, and corporate lawyer who had successfully navigated the (supposedly) ultra-left-wing world of Silicon Valley. And unlike fellow Yalie Buckley, the son of a millionaire, Vance really was from a hardscrabble background. If anything, the liberal establishment took his story as proof that the American political and economic system fundamentally worked. Vance's argument that white rural poverty stemmed from a culture of laziness and welfare dependency simply took age-old racialized tropes about Black and brown people and redirected them to poor whites. For all of the establishment's gushing that *Hillbilly Elegy* explained Trumpism, Vance offered largely bog-standard Republicanism and was completely embraced by liberal elites. Not even Buckley got a Ron Howard movie.

What is novel—at least so far—about Vance's political trajectory is that unlike Buckley or Reagan, who began as "radicals" and morphed into "responsible conservatives" as far as liberals were concerned, Vance has traveled the opposite direction. At one time he might have made a political name for himself by running as a moderate Republican or even a conservative Democrat—a millennial Joe Manchin. But there is little future in national politics today for either moderate Republicans or conservative Democrats.

In reality, Vance was never very far from the far right. His mentor in Silicon Valley circles was Peter Thiel, among the most influential right-wing power brokers in American politics today. Thiel's first book, published well before he became a billionaire, was entitled *The Diversity Myth: Multiculturalism and the Politics of Intolerance at Stanford*, and in 2009—years before Vance joined his orbit—he wrote that he no longer believed that "freedom and democracy are compatible." As for Vance's populist rhetoric in July at the Republican National Convention, which some commentators have interpreted as signaling a shift toward a pro-worker Republican Party, the truth is that it resembled nothing so much as the antimonopolist rhetoric of the far-right John Birch Society and the Liberty Lobby in the

1970s. For that matter, the rhetoric of producers versus parasites is entirely within keeping of the arguments of *Hillbilly Elegy*.

Vance cannily understands that national political hegemony has flipped *again*, at least in the liberal narrative. It is no longer the age of Reagan; it is the age of Trump. And while Vance's speech to the RNC was full of dangerous and illiberal overtones—especially on birthrates and immigration—there is little political price to be paid over the long term for one's image as "responsible," provided that you can back it up with political victory. If Vance can convince liberals again that he knows a secret—and that if they could learn the secret from him again, they, too, could be as popular as he—then there is no reason to think that he could not once again be fashioned as a "responsible conservative." Because it is ultimately liberals who make that determination.

MAPPING INJURY

*Sunaura Taylor interviewed by Rebecca
Tuhus-Dubrow*

SUNAURA TAYLOR's first book, *Beasts of Burden* (2017), was praised
for its novel exploration of the links between disability studies and
animal rights. Taylor, who uses a wheelchair and has limited arm
mobility, sympathized with the plight of factory-farmed animals
from an early age. "If animal and disability oppression are entangled," she wrote, "might not that mean their paths of liberation are
entangled as well?"

In her new book, *Disabled Ecologies*, Taylor finds both overlap
and tension between disability studies and environmental justice. She
grew up with the understanding that her own disability came from
contaminated groundwater on the south side of Tucson, where her
family had moved when her mother was pregnant with her. Military
contractors—particularly Hughes Aircraft, which later merged with
Raytheon, now called RTX—had dumped toxic waste into unlined
lagoons; the area was eventually designated as a Superfund site. In
the '70s and '80s, the community noticed patterns of disproportionate

illness and disability; they organized, forming Tucsonans for a Clean Environment—one of the earliest environmental justice groups in the country.

Taylor's family left Arizona when she was five, but in 2018 she returned to Tucson to investigate what happened there and get to know the community activists. She found that "while they told stories of often debilitating and sometimes life-ending injuries, they also clearly mapped out alternative modes of connection, solidarity, and resistance." In a remarkably fertile inquiry, Taylor takes insights from disability studies and environmental justice and arrives at new revelations that enrich both movements—while also applying far beyond them, to our whole impaired and magnificent planet.

I spoke with Taylor recently by Zoom from her office in Berkeley, where she is an assistant professor of environmental studies. Our conversation has been edited for length and clarity.

—Rebecca Tuhus-Dubrow

Rebecca Tuhus-Dubrow: To start, can you talk about your personal experience and how it drew you to write this book?

Sunaura Taylor: I didn't go into this wanting to write a memoir—the book is not a memoir—but my personal story is so important to the project because it offered me, growing up, a way of thinking about disability and the environment together. I understood that disability wasn't just my own individual medical problem, but something profoundly political that can impact a whole community and can be caused by systems of harm and exploitation—war and pollution and environmental racism.

I also had an understanding that nature isn't separate from us, something out there, but that humans are part of nature—inseparable from it. I had a deep, visceral understanding that injury to the environment is injury to people. These insights are the kinds of things that would later shape my perspectives on disability and the environment. I wanted my next project to make the case for the importance of bringing disability into the environmental conversation. It made sense to me to return to Tucson and root my exploration in the place and history that had shaped me both physically and intellectually.

RT-D: Toward the beginning of the book, you have a striking line on the aquifer water that you've always understood to be the cause of your disability: "My feelings toward this water are not of fear or anxiety or anger. They are of solidarity." Can you say more about that response?

ST: Hughes's pollution contaminated the aquifer on Tucson's south side and thus the community's drinking water. It's not an exaggeration to say that I fell in love with the aquifer while I was researching this book, trying to gain a better understanding of what an aquifer is.

The book's central concept of disabled ecologies links injuries to ecosystems and wildlife and what we think of as nature, to the injury of human beings—not only in cases like this that have to do with pollution, but also with the broader climate crisis, the injurious effects of heat waves, fires, and hurricanes for example. So disabled ecologies can be understood as a kind of mapping project, a way of mapping injuries across human and more-than-human entities, to expose the limitations of thinking about human health and environmental health as two separate issues.

In that sense, we were not injured by the aquifer. We were injured by these extremely powerful corporations, by this massive defense industry, and by government policies that allow these kinds of violences to continue to occur. And that's where the sense of solidarity and kinship comes from.

In my research, I found many accounts of wildlife drinking from where the runoff from the pollution-filled lagoons had traveled through the desert washes or had seeped out, and animals would get very sick and die. Early reports from Hughes employees show that they were really disturbed by this, and it spurred some of them to act, to complain. Decades later community organizers would fight for years for the health of both their community and the health of the aquifer. "Look what they did to our aquifer!" was a common refrain I'd hear in the community. I was moved by these expressions of solidarity people were already making.

RT-D: In your first book, you draw connections between animal rights and disability studies. The second book seems like an extension of the first one in some ways. Is that right?

ST: *Beasts of Burden* is exactly as you say—it brings together disability liberation and animal liberation. I was particularly drawn to this because of my own commitments to both movements, but also because of the way disability rights and animal rights have been pitted against each other for a whole variety of reasons. We could look to the long histories of disabled people being animalized or to the way mainstream animal rights movements have long framed veganism, not as a liberation movement but as a lifestyle choice connected to health and physical fitness.

The ways that animal liberation has traditionally been argued for in Western philosophical traditions has really caused a lot of damage. These arguments have often relied on the philosophical exploitation of disabled people—particularly intellectually disabled people—to make their case. This whole framing covered up and distracted from much more important dynamics: speciesism and ableism are entangled, and the movements fighting them actually have a lot to offer each other.

I've always been really interested in how we can utilize the insights of disability movements and disability studies to help us better understand how we are relating to and understanding the more-than-human world. To me, disability is a lived experience, but it's also a political and conceptual frame that has a lot of power in the world. And the concepts of disability, ablebodiedness, and ableism impact the way that we think about nonhuman animals, the way that we treat nonhuman animals, but also the way that we interact with and treat our environments and understand nature. *Disabled Ecologies* is an extension of these ideas—a further exploration of disability beyond the human. How does disability shape our understanding of nature? How is ableism entangled with anthropocentrism and environmental catastrophe?

RT-D: I'm writing a book about nuclear power. During the heyday of the antinuclear movement, one of the greatest fears was that radiation from fallout and nuclear plants would cause heritable genetic diseases and disorders. On the one hand, I understand this fear—people felt like they were at the mercy of a military-industrial complex that could harm them and their children and grandchildren. But as you point out, this kind of fear can be intertwined with a stigmatization of genetic difference and disability. And that's a thorny area to navigate. How do you think about that tension?

ST: I think of it as a paradox of disability. Disability can emerge from exploitative, horrendous things, but there's also this reality that I have experienced—and I know countless others have too—of leading thriving lives in the disability community and as disabled and sick people. There are ways of experiencing the world—values and politics—that emerge from disability that are valuable, that shouldn't just be desired away in some eugenic vision of utopia.

One of my favorite books in disability studies is Alison Kafer's *Feminist, Queer, Crip.* It looks at different visions of "a good future," from radical feminist utopias to much more conservative images, and finds that what they all have in common is an erasure of disability—a good world is a world where no one is sick and no one becomes disabled.

Taylor & Tuhus-Dubrow

That, for me, is not a good world. A eugenicist world is not a good world. Partially, of course, because it's a fantasy—there will always be disability. Disability is an integral phenomenon in nature. The capacity to heal requires the capacity to be injured. And we all age. We all go in and out of vulnerability. It's a fundamental, if sometimes unpleasant, aspect of reality.

But that doesn't mean that I want to support systems that perpetually create disablement and profit off of it. It doesn't mean I'm celebrating disablement. Look at what is happening in Gaza, this utterly horrific mass killing and also mass disablement of people—there is nothing celebratory here. It is horror. So the way that I've come to think about these things is that there's nothing wrong, *of course*, with wanting your community to be healthy, with not wanting to be poisoned and get sick. That is not an ableist position or an antidisability position. That is an anti-injustice position. The challenge to me becomes, how we respond to those human beings, those animals, those environments that do become disabled, that are forced to live with the aftermath of injury? Do we respond with eugenics and ableism or with a politics of disability justice and liberation?

Another scholar who's been really helpful to me in thinking through this question is Nirmala Erevelles. In her 2011 book *Disability and Difference in Global Contexts*, Erevelles asks, "Under what conditions might we welcome disability?" And she suggests that for disability perspectives to be generative, they must first address the conditions—racial capitalism, colonialism, war—that cause so much disablement.

RT-D: You write about the early environmental movement, the conservation movement. A lot of people are aware that it was overwhelmingly white and in some cases racist, but maybe less salient to some people is how ablebodiedness was so integral to it. Early Sierra Club members were all about hiking and rock climbing. That's the prevailing image of what it means to love nature. Your book describes how the connection with nature can take a different form.

ST: Throughout the book I'm interested in what it means to be a disabled person engaging with the genre of nature writing—a genre that historically excluded disabled people. Here I'm indebted again to Kafer, who laid out the ways in which a lot of environmental writing, environmental philosophy, and as you say the environmental movement, often fall back on these tropes of the rugged individual experiencing and connecting to nature through physical feats and aloneness—things that are associated with ablebodiedness, as well as whiteness and class status.

So, what does a crip engagement with nature look like? There is the intimacy born out of shared experience of injury—my own disablement being connected to the disablement of Tucson's aquifer, for example. But I was also thinking more broadly: How do disabled people connect to nature, celebrate, and enjoy nature? I turned to disabled people who were writing about their connection to nature and renarrativizing these stories. There are of course a lot of different ways that disabled people do this, but one throughline I found is a valuing by disabled people of what is not even necessarily consid-

Taylor & Tuhus-Dubrow

ered nature by a society that likes to distinguish between the built environment and what's "natural." As disabled author Naomi Ortiz describes, experiencing nature for those with mobility impairments often means celebrating the edges, the thresholds, the parking lots of nature parks, for example. Nature is of course everywhere, and this kind of connection is built on an understanding that nature is not something that you necessarily have to go to. We can appreciate and care for the nature we are already in. This is of course similar to an environmental justice position—that nature is where we live, work, and play.

Engaging with the genre of nature writing was also interesting to me because the central character, if you will, that I was writing about was an aquifer. An aquifer is not an environment anyone can go to, no matter how physically robust one is, although sadly that doesn't make them any less exploitable than any other natural "resource." Relating to an aquifer is an act of imagination. Crip engagement offers new ways of building connection so that we can realize and think through our responsibilities towards nature.

RT-D: You have a fascinating section about origin stories—the different roles they play and the ways they've been perceived in the disability and environmental justice movements. Why is the question "What happened to you?" not always welcomed by disabled people?

ST: The disability community that I was raised in politically in my twenties and thirties had a resistance to the focus on origin stories because they can distract from the political dynamics that impact disabled people. A sensational story about what happened to you individually distracts from the structural barriers and discrimination and inequities disabled people face living in an ableist society.

Disability studies in that era—I think it's changing now—was also resistant to those kinds of stories because of the ways it separates people. The movement was about building connection across people whose differences made it challenging to define them as a group but who were all nonetheless oppressed by ableism. The category of disability is a cultural and historical category. It doesn't *necessarily* make sense that you'd have blind people in solidarity with people with mental illness or in solidarity with people in wheelchairs or chronic illness. But forging the group identity as a political force was something that disability community and disability studies did.

I would say that, in general, in environmental justice communities it's the opposite. Origin stories are useful to politicize illness and disability. They are a way of saying, not look at what happened to me, but look at what happened to us. Origin stories become a way of exposing systemic racism and corporate malfeasance, for example. Many community members I found would say, *if only* people would ask what happened to us. The question can be an opening to point to evidence of systemic harm and injustice.

I also explore how polluters themselves utilize origin stories—and often they do not tell one at all. So I look at the different work that origin stories do. When is it powerful to tell an origin story, and when is it powerful to not tell one? And how can movements use both choices to work toward common ends—to politicize disability,

Taylor & Tuhus-Dubrow

to push back against individualizing disability, and to show disability's connections to social inequities?

RT-D: Are the conversations that you're trying to encourage between disability and environmental justice movements starting to happen?

ST: I would never suggest that the environmental justice and disability communities have never been in conversation. For one thing, they are often the same community—people for whom these issues were never separate.

But very little has been written about the relationships between these two movements, and a lot of what exists focuses on the tensions or points of departure between them. So one of the things that I wanted to do is explore the points of connection that are already there and pull out those threads.

In terms of the broader environmental movement and disability, in the eight years or so since I started researching for this book, the disability movement has increasingly been grappling with questions of the environment, questions of climate change—no doubt in part because we are seeing again and again the disproportionate death of disabled people during extreme weather events—for example, because emergency and disaster services are too often not trained to evacuate disabled people. The effort to address these things has been deepening in the disability community and disability studies.

But we need more people doing this work because the scale of the problem is just so extraordinary. Working with my students here at UC Berkeley in the Disabled Ecologies Lab gives me hope because they are bringing disability studies and a lived experience of disability to all of these various arenas: climate mitigation, forestry, river ecology, environmental justice.

RT-D: For most of my life, I found it hard to accept that we wouldn't "solve" climate change in my lifetime or maybe ever, or "save" the planet. But now I'm not sure it's helpful to think about it in those terms. I think the world will always be imperfect, to say the least, and we can grieve but we can still find joy and connection. A critical disabilities perspective seems to suggest something similar.

ST: Absolutely. *Disabled Ecologies* has an element of hope, because of this disability paradox we discussed earlier. We see a lot of work right now that says, basically, nature is dead. It's the end of everything. But I think something else is happening and will only increase, which is the ongoing mass disablement of nature. And death is undeniably a part of that. This disablement, to be clear, is not something that I want to romanticize or that I want to have happen. I say it with so much grief and anger that we could let this happen. But I also know that disabled people can live good lives, that disabled people are experts in adapting, in caring, in acknowledging and celebrating vulnerability and interdependence.

And I reiterate this a hundred times in the book—that living with injury has to be connected to a resistance to the systems that are continuing to cause harm. It can't just be an acceptance that this is what we have now, so let's just keep extracting and hoarding and whoever has the most and the best survival skills will survive. No. I know that it is also possible, when we're attentive to challenging the ableist responses to environmental harm, that disabled beings can live good lives. And that, for me, is hopeful.

A Tanzanian 100 shilling banknote. Images: Alamy

THE POLITICS OF PRICE

Kevin P. Donovan

A TERSE TELEGRAM from Dar es Salaam first alerted Barclays Bank in London of the unexpected and immediate nationalization of its local subsidiary in Tanzania. "We are advised full compensation will be paid," said the message, and "government wishes all branches to continue normal business under present management." Yet this was anything but business as usual.

A day earlier, on February 5, 1967, Tanzania's president, Julius Nyerere, had announced the takeover of all "major means of production." This was a cornerstone of his Arusha Declaration, a transformative project of creating *ujamaa na kujitegemea*, or African socialism and self-reliance. Important manufacturing and agricultural industries, as well as land and larger trading firms, were to be placed "under the control and ownership of the Peasants and Workers themselves through their Government and their Co-operatives." So too were the three British banks that had dominated the country's economy since colonial times: National & Grindlays,

Standard Bank, and Barclays Bank D.C.O. (previously, Dominion, Colonial & Overseas).

"Our independence is not yet complete," Nyerere told crowds. Though the country had won independence in 1961, British banks in Tanzania still operated as mere branches of their London offices. Little effort was expended on providing savings accounts to Africans, and lending concentrated on a few agricultural products destined for export. Moreover, the banks shuttled their profits to British shareholders and invested customer deposits and other surplus in London's capital markets. In other words, Tanzania was actually lending Britain money. Prior to nationalization in 1967, foreign banks exported an estimated $4 million annually. In their place a new, government-owned National Bank of Commerce was tasked with using finance in service of national development.

Tanzanians celebrated the Arusha Declaration with patriotic marches across the country. Letters to the editor in the main newspaper, *The Nationalist*, predicted the end of foreign exploitation. Elderly citizens appeared at bank branches to open savings accounts. Within three months of nationalization, bank deposits had increased 30 percent over the previous year.

The expropriations in Tanzania were part of a global wave. Some midcentury nationalization efforts reflected the rise of social democratic parties in Europe: banks and energy companies in France, railways and the Bank of England in Britain. Others were aspects of decolonization. As Christopher Dietrich and Idriss Fofana have shown, postcolonial lawyers, diplomats, and economists successfully justified the expansion of sovereign power into the domain of production, finance, and natural resources. In 1962 the UN General Assembly resolved in favor of the right to expropriate property as long as "appropriate compensation" was paid, declaring that "grounds or reasons of public utility, security or the national interest" were to be recognized as "overriding purely individual or private interests, both domestic and foreign."

After Gamal Abdel Nasser began nationalizing Egyptian banks in 1960, Barclays understood that political independence set the stage for changes in property, ownership, and wealth. As a *Financial Times* columnist wrote after Tanzania's actions, expropriation was an "occupational hazard" but not an existential one. Despite nationalizations in Syria, Burma, and Tanzania, Barclays still had nearly 50 percent more overseas branches in 1967 than it did a decade prior. The bank resented the expropriation of its profitable business, of course, but it begrudgingly accepted its legality. So when Nyerere promised "full and fair compensation," telling journalists that "we must pay the price for our policies," bankers and bureaucrats turned to the question of price. Tanzania could hardly afford to pay very much, yet the British banks held an enormous bargaining chip: Barclays and Standard together held more than £1.5 million of depositors' money in London. British diplomats called it a "ransom," and the bankers refused to remit it until a settlement was reached—a fraught negotiation that took more than two years to resolve.

Accounting is rarely considered the stuff of socialist revolutions, but the case of socialist Tanzania shows how decolonizing the economy quite literally boiled down to correctly calculating prices. At a moment when price controls, inflation, and even nationalization are again at the forefront of public debate, the history of Tanzania's bank nationalization demonstrates why the arcane technicalities of valuation should not be left to managerial elites alone. Today, advocacy groups like Groundwork Collaborative have made corporate pricing decisions a political issue, and economists like Isabella Weber are exploring how systematically significant prices might be calculated and regulated.

Similar insights emerge in sociologist Liliana Doganova's recent, wide-ranging exploration of financial accounting, *Discounting the Future*. As she sharply demonstrates, valuation is a "political technology." Neither a private affair nor an objective lens, it is a tool that produces inequalities of wealth, shapes how property is owned, and determines where investments are made. "No value exists independently from the instrument through which it is measured," she writes. The routing of Tanzanian socialism and self-reliance through arcane debates about accounting techniques is a case in point.

WHAT IS a bank worth? Barclays initially proposed a compensation of nearly £2.5 million. It arrived at the bulk of this figure by projecting past annual profits forward in perpetuity—in particular, by averaging the past two years of profit and dividing that number by an estimate of the so-called capitalization rate ("cap rate"), a valuation technique most often used in real estate.

Barclays argued this was the proper and uncontroversial method for assessing the bank's present value, equivalent to what a "willing buyer" would offer a "willing seller" in an acquisition and "well understood and accepted in business circles throughout the world." In the bank's depiction, such accounting methods were apolitical tools that produced objective facts. The bankers also knew the cap rate valuation did Tanzania no favors. By insisting the formula set the price, they tried to immunize their claims against accusations of self-interest.

The country's negotiators dissented. On what basis could past profits be presumed to continue indefinitely into the future, and how many years of profits should be averaged to account for the past? Barclays chose two years because they had been especially lucrative, but the Tanzanians insisted that such opportunistic enumerations be amended. At best, they argued, the cap rate technique was a rule of thumb. Rather than imbuing it with objectivity, they rightly saw the calculations as political, reminding Barclays that its prior profits were facilitated by the colonial "cartel" agreement that allowed banks to "impose on the public what charges it liked." Moreover, the idea that a compulsory nationalization should be judged by the standard of a market transaction belied the categorical difference: there was no "willing" buyer or seller in the 1967 expropriation.

Tanzania suggested that what it owed all nine nationalized banks, including Barclays, amounted to £900,000. Instead of using the cap rate method, government negotiators relied on a protocol called "net asset value." Also known as "book value," this approach uses the balance sheet of a business to subtract liabilities from assets. Within a matter of months, Tanzania made deals with most of the affected banks, but the big three balked at this approach and refused to fully open their books (perhaps to avoid revealing a history of tax avoidance).

The 1967 nationalization law had made net asset value the law of the land, and the country could honestly say it was a common enough accounting standard around the world. But Barclays held very few assets in Tanzania, in part due to continually exporting profits to London, and by some accounts its assets were actually less than its liabilities. It thus rightly fretted that "compensation received on a net asset basis will be small," limited to items like furniture, vehicles, and stationary. As the bank's chairman put it, "this meant that our 50 years of development and profitable operations were virtually valueless from the point of view of compensation."

Barclays hoped to use financial accounting as an inviolable law of value, but Tanzania's insistence turned the presumed fixity of accounting into a proliferation of discretionary choices. Instead of using either cap rate or book value, Barclays proposed they simply multiply an average of past profits by some fixed number of years. Yet how many years of prior profit should be averaged, and exactly how many years into the future should those historical numbers be expected to prevail? Any formula seemed to contain controversial variables.

While negotiations stalled, Tanzania's new National Bank of Commerce got busy remaking finance anyway. It closed duplicate branches, eliminated the expensive salaries paid to British managers, and stopped capital from leaking out of the country. In its first six months of operation, NBC reported making £300,000—not bad for an entity widely expected to collapse immediately. In the longer term, NBC worked to end a history of credit discrimination, expand banking to citizens, and balance short-run profitability against developmental goals.

When negotiations finally resumed in mid-1968, the parties agreed to focus on finding a suitable final price to be paid instead of fighting over the minutiae of financial formulas. As Tanzania's lead negotiator, J. D. Namfua, acknowledged, if each side was simply changing their variables "to achieve a pre-determined result, we are not engaged in a process of valuation, but in the vulgar business of bargaining." By early 1969, the sides settled near £1 million, far below Barclays' opening proposal. For Tanzania it was still a large number, but it could seem like a rather good deal combined with the return of nearly £700,000 held hostage in London. Nyerere was delighted to sign the agreement in June 1969, fulfilling the promises he made to both citizens and foreigners on that February day two years prior.

By the time Tanzania turned political authority into economic sovereignty, similar examples of large-scale nationalization had peppered the globe, from Guatemala and Argentina to Egypt, Iran, and Indonesia. As Quinn Slobodian and Adom Getachew have both traced, the threat national liberation posed to multinational ownership was a key motivation for the neoliberal counterrevolution of the late twentieth century. Against the rights of citizens to reshape markets, neoliberals asserted the rights of owners to constrain citizens, and in doing so they transformed the law surrounding nationalization. What was once managed politically through case-by-case negotiations—as in Tanzania—is now routed through depoliticized forums and dominated by financial methods that are insulated from scrutiny.

Among the most significant such moves are the investment treaties that move compensation claims out of national jurisdiction and into international arbitration panels. Since 1966, the World Bank has taken the leading role in promoting and overseeing this form of parallel justice, in the process sidelining what might have been more equitable alternatives like investor insurance. By the 1980s, the World Bank and International Monetary Fund were demanding acquiescence to international arbitration as part of structural adjustment programs. Legal scholar Nicolás Perrone reports that over 1,500 international investment treaties were signed in the heady days of capitalist globalization: four per day between 1994 and 1996. This regime of so-called investor-state dispute settlement (ISDS) emerged from the frustrations of expropriated banks, oil companies, and other multinationals. Today, it works to further their interests and constrain national sovereignty.

During the Barclays negotiations in Tanzania, domestic law prevailed over international law—most notably in grounding the government's use of net asset value—and both political and ethical arguments shaped how accounting was used. In contrast, international arbitration now heightens the influence of financial models and limits the latitude of national governments by expanding the types of behavior that triggers compensation. Even legitimate regulation, such as legislating the phaseout of coal power plants or some types of taxation, might be seen as "indirect expropriation" or a violation of the obligation of "fair and equitable treatment." The arbitration tribunals are staffed by technocrats who are meant to be independent, but in practice their work protects investors (especially in extractive industries).

One way it does so is through the promotion of certain valuation techniques, which have wildly inflated the cost governments must pay for nationalizations. The amounts awarded in recent years have been staggering: $5.8 billion against Pakistan and $8.7 billion against Venezuela in 2019, for instance. Instead of funding schools or hospitals, Pakistan pays foreign mining companies (including Canada's Barrick Gold) and Venezuela owes oil extractors (like Houston's ConocoPhillips).

Legal scholar Toni Marzal has detailed this rise of a theory of compensation that is equal parts peculiar and aggressive. Since the 1990s, arbitration tribunals have not only come to embrace the belief that compensation must be full and at the "fair market value." They also now insist on establishing this value through a financial model known as "discounted cash flow" (DCF), which totally ignores mitigating factors—such as historical harms, or a government's ability to pay, or next year's shift in interest rates. Despite the patina of objectivity, DCF accounting is riven by uncertainties and artifice. While it claims to replicate what an expropriated business would sell for in a real market, its models do not capture the risks, volatility, and imperfections of the real world. In some cases, the compensation paid is more money than the business could sell for in a private transaction. In Pakistan, the enormous sum was awarded to a mining consortium, Tethyan Copper, even though it had not yet obtained necessary authorization, let alone begun operations.

Tanzania had the good fortune of negotiating before the neoliberal transformation, when discretion was allowed to prevail on both sides. (It mattered that Barclays did not wish to sully its reputation or bankrupt Tanzania by pushing for too much.) Today that discretion has been outsourced to arbitrators who disavow their own subjective power. States may still legally nationalize property, but doing so comes with financial costs few wish to shoulder. The result, Marzal argues, is a widespread disregard for other legal principles, including justice and equity. Instead, valuation is "governed entirely by economic and financial logic."

DCF IS AT the core of Doganova's book, which might be read as a biography of discounting. Raised in the scientific forestry of nineteenth-century Germany, discounting matured as a method of twentieth-century managerialism, and today it quietly dominates a huge range of domains, from climate policy to pharmaceutical pipelines and government regulations. While it has critics—on the left, to be sure, but also in business schools—they have largely failed to check its influence. More than just a financial instrument, discounting is now a worldview.

Doganova details the manifold problems of discounting but also emphasizes its mutability. "It can be and do many different, even opposite, things," she writes. Yet the lesson is not that we need merely to revise its protean calculations in hopes of guiding more decent behavior. We need both to rework valuation formulas and to subordinate them to more justifiable principles.

But just what is discounting? With compound interest, a dollar today can multiply to considerably more in the course of ten, twenty, or more years. Discounting turns this idea around, advising that if you know you are going to bear a certain cost in the future—like building a wall in 2050 to rebuff higher sea levels—you should only be willing to pay considerably less to deal with it in the present. After all, you could use your money today for other purposes, presumably getting richer and more sophisticated before you must deal with that future problem. As Doganova explains, "money expected in the future is equivalent to 'less money today,' because this 'less money today' is supposed to be able to produce that 'more money in the future.'"

For discounting's adherents, this logic means that you may see an expensive looming problem—due to climate change, for instance, or carcinogenic waste—as unworthy of investment today because its "discounted present value" is too high. These calculations depend not only on the time horizon and the estimated future cost. What matters most of all is the discount *rate*—the factor by which future costs should be diminished to get present value—and there is simply no objective way of determining what the "right" rate should be. In practice, the rate chosen varies hugely from analyst to analyst. Rather than a hard and fast science, a discount rate is a political and moral choice, and whatever number is selected takes on magnified significance when compounded across the years.

Along with related methods like "net present value," DCF is among the most influential means of deciding how investments are made. Confronted with a range of options—from buying back stock to opening a new factory—corporate managers will calculate how much they can comparatively expect to earn over a given timeline. Some critics argue that discounting encourages a short-term outlook.

Harvard Business School professors in the 1980s, for instance, claimed that discounting's widespread use was encouraging insufficient capital investment, trading long-term productivity for short-term returns. Indeed, the evolution of discounting in those decades was a key driver of financialization and industrial outsourcing—a large obstacle to today's effort to rebuild U.S. manufacturing.

Governments, too, have adopted discounting to guide their actions. Foucault was among the first to notice. His 1978–79 lectures depicted accounting principles as an "economic grid" used to judge the worthiness of government actions and "object to activities of the public authorities on the grounds of their abuses, excesses, futility, and wasteful expenditure." On this logic, what counts as wasteful or abusive is routed through the discount rate. Sometimes, the result is shocking: in the early 1980s, the U.S. Office of Management and Budget (OMB) followed the discounting math to argue against regulating asbestos because the resulting cancer would only emerge in forty years, significantly lowering the cost to the present. The scandal wasn't only that the OMB used discounting against the Environmental Protection Agency's preferences; it was that the OMB chose a high discount rate without meaningful justification. The result is emblematic of what many critics decry as a disregard for the future.

For proponents, however, the tool is useful precisely to account for the future. After all, its key insight is that value must be a *temporal* judgment of money. As Doganova traces, the early formulations of discounting arose in commercial forestry to balance present output with the future viability of the forest. Rather than judging a forest through the current price of wood, the new science of forestry emphasized the future flows of costs and revenues, appropriately discounted for the present. In practice, this encouraged earlier felling, but it kept an eye on the forest as future trees, as well.

Yet getting too hung up on the question of the future risks obscuring the consequences for the present. In nineteenth-century Germany, discounting pitted the poor who depended on collecting wood against the forest owners and their state allies who criminalized gleaning. Doganova reports that in the Spessart region, "one out of ten inhabitants stood trial every year for committing a forest offense." A young Karl Marx observed in 1842 that commercial and government foresters worked together to expel the commoners in order to maintain present *and* future capitalist value. The poor's need for fuel became illegitimate as the "forest as wood" was refigured as "forest as capital." As Doganova explains, the present profitability of forestry as well as its future viability led to expulsion of the poor in that moment.

In other words, it would be misleading to see discounting as a straightforward economization of the state. Its impact is more unexpected than that, and it often depends on the alliance between accommodating states and large firms.

Consider Chile, where DCF was legally enshrined as part of Augusto Pinochet's counterrevolution against socialist Salvador Allende. As Doganova details, it took a shift in sovereign power and constitutional law to make discounting the *raison d'être*. The key figure is economist José Piñera, one of the Chicago Boys, who served as mining minister after Pinochet's 1973 coup.

Copper mines had been at the center of Allende's economic transformation, and when he nationalized them in 1971, he shared the view of Tanzania's government that foreign firms should be compensated through "book value." But he went further, deducting their "excess profits" as a matter of justice and sovereignty. The result was a compensation payment of zero. When Richard Nixon learned of Allende's math, he told Henry Kissinger, "Allende . . . is really screwing us now. . . . I'm goin' to kick 'em. And I want to make something out of it."

Not two years later, Pinochet had seized power, undoing many of Allende's policies and brutally repressing resistance. But Piñera believed that privatizing the mines would unleash more resistance than even Pinochet could manage. His still aimed to liberalize the country's mining economy, but instead of forcing a change of ownership, he turned to the depoliticized realm of contracts and discounting. First, mining corporations were granted an indefinite concessionary contract to exploit the country's resources. Second, a 1981 law required that any expropriation involve compensation according to DCF—effectively an insurance policy guaranteeing future revenue, even if the concessionary contract might be ended. Piñera thus "granted investors not ownership of the present," Doganova writes, "but control over the future." Expropriation could even be seen as a relief: in the event a company was nationalized, it would get paid without having to do any digging at all.

Chile appears to be the first case where discounting was legally established to protect foreign investors, and it remains on the books in Chile today. Even if the government wanted to capture the future revenue of its mines through nationalization—a right enshrined by the UN in 1962—it would immediately have to pay out those earnings in compensation. Marzal calls such a straightjacket a "mockery"—but it became the standard way of compensating companies after nationalization.

THE HISTORY of discounting makes clear not only how consequential accounting standards can be—bankrupting some, enriching others— and how power inheres in mundane, technical protocols masquerading as value-neutral. It also exposes the critical role of the state in imposing some accounting standards over alternatives. Barclays was unable to enforce its own enrichment at the hands of Tanzanians precisely because the nation had become politically independent in 1961. Pinochet's government was able to secure the profitability of mining corporations precisely because the neoliberals wielded state law. Arbitration panels, too, operate through treaties, acts, and other legal instruments. In each case, law combined with accountancy works to leverage ownership, turning assets into revenue.

What does this merger of law and accounting mean for politics? Doganova argues that discounting's significance lies less in the truth value of accounting than the specific consequences of a calculation being deemed persuasive. After all, financial practitioners are among the most alert to the basic uncertainty surrounding the value of a new drug or factory; it is partly because of this uncertainty that future revenue is discounted in the present. What really matters, in other words, is not so much that the formula produces "truth." What financiers want is for the formula to be *accepted*. We should therefore see financial arithmetic as something like an act of rhetoric: marshalling certain evidence for the means of argumentation and persuasion. When two companies deploy various valuation methods in a commercial acquisition, with their accounts open as part of due diligence, both sides know there is no ironclad set of variables and formulas that would yield an uncontroversial price. Compelled by this result or that, they negotiate before being persuaded and coming to a deal.

The trouble arises when discounting methodologies are deployed with political consequences without inviting the public to the negotiating table. As a style of argumentation, this is a far cry from an ideal of public deliberation, where public opinion and moral values work to legitimate state action. Today, the use of discounting interferes with public reasoning, short-circuiting democratic governance. The privatization of so much of political consequence means that accounting decisions with wider importance never reach the public arena. Drug discovery is a case in point: when pharmaceutical executives decide to invest in profitable interventions for the wealthy, they sacrifice the health of the global poor. Pharma executives may not be fooled by the ultimately speculative nature of the formulas they use, but guided by discounted cash flows—and not the right to health or global justice—their own persuasion undermines public purpose.

Even in cases where democratic mechanisms are ostensibly at play, the resort to accounting can obscure just how arbitrary the formulas are. Pseudo-objective valuation techniques do not only establish worth; they justify it. In concert with what Elizabeth Popp Berman calls the "economic style of reasoning," discounting turns questions of justice into calculations of costs. Climate change is perhaps the preeminent example, where the use of questionable discount rates has encouraged policymakers to underplay the contemporary costs of spewing carbon—part of what Geoff Mann dubs the "new denialism." In a host of other arenas, the deference to technocrats and their financial models means discretionary parameters take on outsized influence. This state of affairs calls for more progressive ways of assessing worth and establishing value—financial value, yes, but also the sorts of values so often colonized by finance.

INSIDE PROJECT 2025

James Goodwin

This essay appeared online in July. In the weeks since, Donald Trump distanced his presidential campaign from Project 2025—culminating in a report, released as this issue went to press, that the initiative's director will leave the Heritage Foundation and that it will cease its policy work. Exactly what these developments mean for the conservative movement remains to be seen, but it would be a mistake to assume this agenda has been drained of its power or significance. The project involved some of the right's most influential leaders—including Stephen Miller and Russell Vought—as well as more than 100 groups throughout the United States. They have made their plans clear, and we should take them seriously. Indeed, implementation of two of the project's pillars—identifying and training potentially thousands of conservatives to work in a future administration—has already begun.

—James Goodwin

THE WEEK AFTER taking office in 2017, Donald Trump announced his administration's signature policy on the administrative state—the constellation of agencies, institutions, and procedures that Congress has created to help the president implement the laws it passes—when he signed Executive Order 13771. The directive purported to create a "regulatory budget" scheme that prohibited agencies from issuing a new rule unless they first repealed two existing rules *and* ensured that the resulting cost savings offset any costs the new rule might impose.

The effort failed. While federal agencies reduced their regulatory output during the Trump administration, they made little lasting progress in repealing existing rules. The Administrative Procedure Act, which governs much of how the administrative state operates, makes it hard to do so. Most of the Trump administration's repeal attempts were met with rejection by federal courts for failing to abide by basic procedural requirements.

Still, Executive Order 13771 perfectly encapsulated conservative thinking about regulatory policy at the time. The goal was to bring about the "deconstruction of the administrative state," as former Trump advisor Steve Bannon famously put it. This view was in keeping with decades of conservative hostility for this arm of government, which the right has long tarred as an economic and constitutional disaster.

But that was then. In the years since, the conservative movement has coalesced around a very different way of thinking about the administrative state—one that sees it as a vehicle for advancing the conservative movement's agenda, particularly on social issues, and thus embraces policy changes that would *strengthen* many aspects of its governing apparatus. There's still plenty of room for deconstruction in this vision, particularly when it comes to issues like worker rights and environmental protection. Indeed, the Supreme Court's conservatives demonstrated their continued commitment to the deconstruction project with their recent decision striking down the four-decade-old *Chevron* deference doctrine, which will make it easier for conservative federal judges to strike down rules they oppose on ideological grounds. But these goals are now presented alongside calls for things like enhanced agency enforcement capacity and strategies for evading congressional oversight—priorities that would have been unthinkable for a conservative regulatory agenda just a few years ago.

The best example of this shift is Project 2025, the Heritage Foundation–led "presidential transition" attack plan that would guide a second Trump administration should he win this November. The effort was spearheaded by Heritage president Kevin Roberts in 2022; a 920-page document called *Mandate for Leadership*, published in April last year, sets out a comprehensive blueprint in technocratic detail. The product of a broad coalition of ultra-right-wing think tanks and advocacy organizations, the plan has contributions from the Center for Renewing America (an organization committed to promoting Christian nationalism), Susan B. Anthony Pro-Life America (a prominent group fighting reproductive rights), and FreedomWorks (the Koch-founded organization responsible for mainstreaming the Tea Party agenda, which has since dissolved but nevertheless helped lay the foundation for the conservative movement's evolution in thinking on matters of regulatory policy). It covers nearly every policy issue you can think of, from defense budgets to bank regulation to highway construction. (For his part, Bannon has expressed generalized support for the initiative, but it is unclear whether he appreciates—or even cares about—the shift it represents.)

Project 2025 is candid about its ultimate goal: to reprogram the U.S. administrative state to support and sustain archconservative rule for decades to come. The distinguishing features of this regime would include a far more politicized bureaucracy, immunity against meaningful public or congressional oversight, abusive deployment of agency enforcement capabilities as a tool of political retribution, and aggressive manipulation of federal program implementation in the image of Christian nationalism, white supremacy, and economic inequality.

ONE OF THE *Mandate*'s prevailing themes is that the administrative state has become a major platform from which the radical left is able to smuggle its "woke" agenda into nearly every nook and cranny of our society. In light of this alleged shift, Project 2025 concludes that deconstruction is no longer the right strategy. Instead, the administrative state must be aggressively harnessed and then redirected. This is not a brand-new idea; conservatives have weaponized the administrative state to fight culture wars in the past, including putting arbitrary regulations on abortion clinics and introducing stringent eligibility requirements for food assistance programs. But these experiments have largely been episodic and disjointed. Project 2025's novelty lies in the fact that it wants to make them, for the first time, into a comprehensive strategy.

Russell Vought, Trump's former Director of the Office of Management and Budget (OMB), succinctly describes this new strategy in a chapter he wrote for *Mandate for Leadership*: "The great challenge confronting a conservative President is the existential need for aggressive use of the vast powers of the executive branch to return power—including power currently held by the executive branch—to the American people." Doing so, the *Mandate* argues, requires giving a second Trump administration nearly unchecked power over the machinery by which the administrative state operates: the institutions, the procedures, the resources, and the personnel.

Project 2025 is clearly designed to avoid the pitfalls that doomed Executive Order 13771. In many ways, *Mandate for Leadership* can be read as an instruction manual for undermining the safeguards meant to prevent governing officials from engaging in the abuses of power Project 2025 wants to encourage. Replete with methodical detail and technocratic jargon, it offers future political leadership across all the federal administrative agencies a full taxonomy of tactics they can deploy to either exploit the weak points in these safeguards or bypass them altogether.

One of the *Mandate*'s central tactics concerns rules around staffing. Currently, agencies hire professional career staff with specialized training and expertise. All must swear an oath to follow the Constitution in carrying out their duties—even and especially if that means disobeying the orders of someone higher up in the bureaucratic hierarchy. As such, these career staff provide perhaps the most important line of defense against an autocratic presidential regime. But through a policy called Schedule F, the *Mandate* seeks to sideline or even purge them. Derived from another of Trump's executive orders, the proposal would reclassify the thousands of career government employees who play some role in policy formation outside of the competitive service—the federal personnel category that includes rigorous, merit-based requirements for hiring, firing, and promotion decisions. Stripped of these basic protections, which have been in place for over 140 years, many employees would become "at will," fireable for any reason—or no reason at all. The intent is obvious: to encourage public servants to obey their political bosses, even when that means going against the law and their own expertise. Were it to take effect, workers who refuse to toe the line could be summarily terminated.

And to buttress the effect of Schedule F, *Mandate for Leadership* includes several more targeted methods for isolating recalcitrant public servants. Its chapter on the intelligence community, for instance, describes policy changes that would make it easier to suspend or revoke security clearances for career staff at national security–related agencies. Without their security clearances, these individuals would no longer be able to perform their jobs—and that, of course, is the point. Other sections contemplate taking similarly hostile actions against members of the Senior Executive Service, a special band within the civil service created to serve as a bridge between political appointees and lower-line career staff by providing management support and expertise. Members who step out of line might find themselves being relocated to far-flung geographic locations or reassigned to positions unrelated to their area of expertise.

THE FLIPSIDE OF silencing or firing career public servants is to empower extremists and amplify outlier viewpoints—a move *Mandate for Leadership* has plenty of ideas about how to accomplish. One of these is simply to point Schedule F and security clearance abuses in the opposite direction. Unburdened by the competitive hiring process, agencies could hire whomever they wanted for career civil service positions. Project 2025 makes clear that unquestioned loyalty to the president, as opposed to professionalism and expertise, is the only real qualification that matters. Similarly, political appointees would have a freer hand to assign security clearances, ensuring loyal voices are heard loud and clear when it comes to conducting intelligence assessments to inform national security decisions.

Mandate for Leadership at times even directly requires consideration of outlier views. One of its recommendations to "improve" the President's Daily Briefing (PDB) on national security issues is to create a mechanism that ensures the inclusion of "properly channeled dissent." *Mandate* fails to specify what constitutes a proper channel, but the broader context of the recommendation indicates a hostility toward the independent viewpoints of career intelligence officers as well as a desire to transform these documents from objective analyses into advocacy documents.

Another group of proposed tactics builds on the longstanding conservative tradition of outsourcing critical government functions to the private sector. Even here, though, the goal isn't simply to shrink government but to advance Project 2025's broader ideological agenda as well. The chapter on the Department of Energy, for instance, urges consideration of outsourcing the functions of the Energy Information Administration (EIA), a small statistical agency charged with gathering and analyzing data regarding U.S. energy systems. The information products that the EIA generates are crucial for informing energy-related policymaking and investments by the electricity and oil and gas sectors; it is perhaps best known for the different "outlooks" it publishes that forecast future energy trends. While conceding that the EIA's products are generally "neutral"—if anything, the agency's outlooks have been criticized for being too pessimistic about renewable energy—*Mandate* still suggests that the reform could be beneficial overall by reducing the costs of government. Previous experience with privatization casts doubt on this prediction. More troubling still, businesses interested in securing future lucrative contracts might deliberately produce analyses that align with the president's preferred policy positions on energy. A future president opposed to urgent climate action, for instance, might be able to use biased analyses to oppose policies aimed at promoting renewable energy development.

Mandate for Leadership elsewhere calls for dismantling the National Oceanic and Atmospheric Administration's (NOAA) lifesaving weather forecasting capabilities and outsourcing them to private companies. Such a move could exacerbate economic and racial inequity if the private company were to put those forecasts— which are now freely available to everyone—behind a paywall that might be unaffordable for many families. More ominously still, a company responding to profit incentives might create what amounts to a two-tier forecasting system, with more accurate forecasts available only for wealthier parts of the country. Low-quality forecasts in poorer areas would leave residents unable to plan for the kind of extreme weather conditions that are becoming more prevalent with climate change, putting their lives and property at risk of unnecessary harm.

Alongside its calls for expanded privatization, *Mandate for Leadership* advocates for politicizing existing relationships with contractors. Its chapter on the U.S. Agency for International Development (USAID), for instance, recommends that the agency end its reliance on "global [non-governmental organizations]" such as Oxfam International for distributing humanitarian assistance, and instead turn the work over to "faith-based organizations," including both local churches as well as larger U.S.-based organizations such as Catholic Relief Services and Knights of Columbus—the perfect vehicles for indoctrinating aid recipients in the conservative Christian ideology that is at Project 2025's core.

Previously, the Trump administration used these humanitarian assistance programs as leverage to induce recipient countries to join the infamous Geneva Consensus Declaration on Promoting Women's Health and Strengthening the Family (GCD). The international agreement, developed outside of any recognized international governance structures such as the United Nations, binds signatory countries in adopting domestic and foreign policies that oppose abortion. Consistent with these neocolonial aspirations, *Mandate for Leadership* strongly embraces the GCD, envisioning the use of humanitarian aid programs implemented by faith-based organization contractors to expand its reach to new countries.

More generally, *Mandate for Leadership* calls for weaponizing contractor policy against companies with "woke" policies. Come 2025, a company that has adopted certain kinds of Diversity, Equity, Inclusion, and Justice (DEIJ) programs might find itself ineligible for many federal grant opportunities. The chapter on the Department of Education would prohibit public schools that receive federal assistance from entering contracts with companies that recognize transgender people's pronouns—a set of policies that would complement recently adopted legislation in conservative states that prohibit DEIJ programs in public institutions of higher education.

Mandate for Leadership also contains several recommendations for how agencies could weaponize federal grantmaking to advance conservative policy objectives. For instance, the chapter on the Department of Health and Human Services recommends that the Teen Pregnancy Prevention and Personal Responsibility Education programs prioritize grants for abstinence-only programs. The chapter on the Environmental Protection Agency calls for radically overhauling that agency's grants program, which distributes hundreds of millions of dollars in discretionary grants every year. *Mandate* would end the practice of career staff making these grant determinations and instead assign this task to a "political appointee."

PERHAPS THE MOST disquieting category of tactics in *Mandate for Leadership* involves the aggressive, politicized use of agency enforcement powers. The chapter on the Department of Justice (DOJ) proposes overhauling the agency to eliminate its longstanding tradition of political insulation from the White House. In theory, this insulation follows from the idea that the job of the DOJ's head, the attorney general, is to represent the U.S. government and not the president. Institutional mechanisms have been used to ensure the agency's independence and to guard against both the perception and reality of conflicts of interest, including, most notably, the use of a special counsel to investigate and prosecute the president or certain administration officials. As was demonstrated during the first Trump term, though, the actual independence of a special counsel can be limited. *Mandate* would seek to further degrade the DOJ's independence by injecting greater presidential control into questions of litigation strategy, even raising the disturbing specter of the president targeting political enemies with enforcement actions.

Likewise, in its chapter on the Department of Homeland Security, the document outlines various proposals aimed at consolidating and strengthening enforcement policies at U.S. Immigration and Customs Enforcement. These include giving individual agents greater leeway to arrest immigrants with suspected criminal records and expanding the geographic scope of Expedited Removal procedures—the summary removal of noncitizens without a hearing. *Mandate* would permit these procedures to be applied to individuals more than 100 miles from the U.S.-Mexico border, which was the traditional limit, with no apparent bright-line geographic restrictions.

Project 2025 also envisions expanded use of the Insurrection Act of 1807, which authorizes the president to use the military for domestic law enforcement purposes under rare, extreme circumstances. In

2020, Trump threatened to use this authority to quell the Black Lives Matter protests that took place in the wake of George Floyd's murder before being discouraged from doing so by his advisors. *Mandate for Leadership*, while not citing the law by name, does appear to endorse its use as part of its broader border control strategy, recommending calling in "active-duty military personnel and National Guardsmen to assist in arrest operations along the border—something that has not yet been done." Citing internal documents and an anonymous source, the *Washington Post* has reported that key personnel involved in Project 2025 have plans to use the Insurrection Act even beyond what *Mandate for Leadership* lays out for it.

Mandate for Leadership's final set of tactics for hijacking the administrative state have to do with limiting or evading congressional oversight. Several chapters, for instance, describe how the administration can manipulate the Federal Vacancies Reform Act by installing political appointees in key agency leadership positions—a gambit whose practical effect is to enable politically loyal personnel to carry out official agency business without being subjected to the lengthy, and potentially embarrassing, Senate confirmation process.

Other chapters recommend giving the president greater control over communications between agencies and committees of jurisdictions with Congress, with the apparent aim of controlling the flow of information that members of Congress and their staff receive. Instituting these changes would clearly undermine Congress's ability to conduct meaningful oversight for these agencies. The chapter on the DHS, for example, calls for the president to demand that only one committee in each chamber serve as an authorizing committee for the agency (currently there are at least six authorizing committees in the House and four more in the Senate). If congressional leadership refuses to accept this arrangement, then it recommends that the agency's Office of Legislative Affairs select one and restrict its communications to only that committee. Similarly, the chapter on the Department of State recommends that agencies defer to the White House on relevant communications with Congress—meaning that in practice, discussions on certain issues of agency business would have to first go through the president.

CONGRESS AND THE federal judiciary have long been ripe for capture by elite minority factions to serve and sustain their rule. But the administrative state, which is of a much more recent vintage, was supposed to be different.

In the years following the Civil War, and then later during the Progressive Era, reformers and advocates sought to build a governing institution that would be more inclusive and democratically responsive. The Interstate Commerce Commission and other early experiments in federal regulatory governance demonstrated that the administrative state could stand up to powerful economic interests and ensure a fairer marketplace for consumers and small businesses while protecting democracy against ever-evolving oligarchic threats. Meanwhile, rapid industrialization and urbanization laid bare the limitations of using civil lawsuits to address harms from dangerous business practices. Agencies like the Food and Drug Administration, first created in 1906, offered the promise of using standards developed and implemented by scientists and other experts to prevent such harms from occurring in the first place. These and other regulatory frameworks created by Congress established a new model in which agencies would be empowered to continually respond to new and emerging threats.

The genius of the administrative state's design was that it would provide a permanent forum in which public input and professional expertise could be leveraged to solve the people's problems in ways that elected officials would, or could, not. Scholars of U.S. democracy have long recognized its potential to serve as a platform for building and sustaining true, durable public power: at its best, they argue, it can provide ordinary citizens with a locus of countervailing power in the political marketplace. It's clear, then, why the modern conservative movement has come to see it as such a threat.

And that is the real import of Project 2025: it seeks to corrupt the administrative state by transforming it from a dynamic base of democratic power into a fierce weapon of social and economic conservatism. What will happen if it succeeds? Once the damage has been done, the task of sustaining minority rule for decades to come would be much easier for the conservative movement. Degrading the institutions of Congress and the federal judiciary were important first steps toward rebuilding the United States in line with its vision of Christian nationalist principles, white supremacy, and economic inequality. Seizing control of the administrative state would be the real prize.

Lyndon B. Johnson and Lady Bird Johnson visit the Fletcher family in Inez, Kentucky, in 1964. Image: Getty Images

GRIEVING IN RURAL AMERICA
Elizabeth Catte

SIXTY YEARS AGO, *Life* photographer John Dominis traveled to eastern Kentucky, where he captured shocking and raw photographs of deprivation—the target of President Lyndon Johnson's recently announced "unconditional war on poverty." Published in a feature photo-essay, the images humanized those who stood to gain the most from new federal aid programs.

The magazine minced no words describing the "dismal" quality of life in Kentucky. Some images show small cabins and homesteads dotting the landscape, ruined by the coal industry, like settlements on a hostile planet. Perhaps most painfully memorable are the more intimate images, taken in bedrooms and sitting rooms, featuring the faces of sick babies and young mothers. Here is a world, the viewer might think, totally inhospitable to life.

Many of the subjects Dominis captured—all of them white— were already on welfare or other available forms of assistance. But this aid proved insufficient when stacked against the economic collapse ravaging Appalachia as strip mining led to layoffs and further devastated the environment. The solution, the Johnson administration proposed, was job retraining, more education, and new infrastructure. Until welfare joined these more vital programs, *Life* argued, all Appalachians could hope to endure was "a life that protects them from starvation but deprives them of self-respect and hope."

Four months later, Johnson traveled to the region himself, and this time an unemployed former coal miner and sawmill operator, Tom Fletcher, became the unwitting face of the campaign. In an iconic photograph published in *Time*, Johnson and Fletcher appear on the steps of Fletcher's small cabin, their contrasting body language and attire a sign of the social distance between them.

The failure of the War on Poverty happened more quietly than its inauguration. In Appalachia, state governments heavily bureaucratized aid, creating disbursement problems and leaving funding vulnerable to siphoning off for other causes. State leaders, often close allies of industry, fomented unrest between "outsiders"—like the young people who served in the initially successful Appalachian Volunteers program—and the people they came to help. In the War on Poverty's wake came successive generations of problem solvers less powerful than the federal government but no less self-assured that their expertise and efforts would set the world right. They also failed. Since the mid-1970s but especially during the Obama years, the Appalachian Regional Commission, created by Congress in 1965, has focused on "public-private partnership" grants and vocational retraining for jobs that don't exist here and aren't particularly well-paid where they do exist. Fletcher never escaped poverty, and neither have his descendants.

Appalachia didn't take center stage in American politics again until the 2016 presidential race, this time anchored to the easy-to-sell but misinformed belief that the region was ground zero for the toxic politics taking root under the banner of Donald Trump. In the months following the publication of J. D. Vance's *Hillbilly Elegy*, a media firestorm insisted that Appalachians—a flimsy proxy for the white working class at large—had declared war on the nation. This narrative had a grain of truth; some blue and purple parts of the region did go solidly red. But it seriously oversold the size and power of Appalachia's electorate compared to other Trump strongholds in well-off cities and suburbs, like Staten Island.

Blissfully, the national media and pundit class declined to drink too deeply from this well during the 2020 race, but the narrative looks set to return with Trump's selection of Vance as his running mate. Since being elected to the Senate from Ohio, Vance has fashioned himself a leader of a new right intelligentsia that is more socially regressive than its predecessors—and in many ways more powerful, thanks to its ties to ultra-wealthy men in tech like Peter Thiel and Marc Andreessen. But if the recent Republican National Convention was any indication, Vance still believes in the power of Appalachia as a political totem. His speech leaned heavily on references to his now-infamous Mamaw and her hillbilly wisdom.

This spells good news for sociologist Arlie Russell Hochschild's new book, *Stolen Pride: Loss, Shame, and the Rise of the Right*. Best known for *Strangers in Their Own Land* (2016), a study of Tea Party members in long-red rural Louisiana, Hochschild now turns her attention to Trump supporters in blue-turned-red Pike County, Kentucky, which is part of the state's 5th congressional district—the whitest and second poorest congressional district in the country—and not far from Breathitt County, where Vance has family roots. Hochschild wants to understand what has fueled the county's rapid lurch to the right since 2008, despite its having gone for Democratic presidents in all but two elections stretching back to 1932.

Stolen Pride joins two other recent books on the politics of poor and rural white people: Reverend William Barber's *White Poverty: How Exposing Myths About Race and Class Can Reconstruct American Democracy*, written with Jonathan Wilson-Hartgrove, and Tom Schaller and Paul Waldman's heavily criticized *White Rural Rage: The Threat to American Democracy*. Each aims to pull apart political messaging and its impact, noting where extremism has been embraced or avoided, and all three venture into the emotional dimension of politics—the way feelings like shame, resentment, dignity, and pride both shape and are shaped by the political landscape.

With Vance now set to reignite the myth of the prodigal son, it matters that we get this narrative right. As Barber most convincingly suggests, it requires recognizing the realities of the lives of poor white Americans, a full accounting of who is to blame, and a genuine path forward.

IN RECENT YEARS, economic precarity and political inertia on recovery plans have only increased in Appalachia. Parts of the region now face almost unsurvivable levels of poverty and its associated diseases of despair, including widespread opioid addiction. Hochschild travels to Pike County in 2018 to try to explain why people experiencing these forces and outcomes have forsaken Democrats and embraced Republicans.

Her answer is what she calls the "pride paradox," the disjuncture between the political choices that dictate the presence or absence "of economic opportunity and one's cultural belief about responsibility for accessing it." In other words, the ideology of individualism—taking full credit for one's successes, but also one's failures—prompts people to see structural failures as their own, which in turn disinclines them from voting for policies that might rein in the savage capitalism decimating the region. Their resulting feelings of shame, Hochschild argues, make them vulnerable to political messaging that encourages them to view their pride as stolen by Democrats.

As a sociologist, Hochschild is best known for exploring the connections between emotions, values, and identity. She takes morality out of the equation, preferring to engage with subjects on their own terms before massaging their stories into a sociological conclusion. In *Stolen Pride*, she borrows the concept of a "deep story" from *Strangers in Their Own Land*: what a person feels to be true, a narrative that operates independently from facts. She sees the post-2020 rhetoric about a stolen election as one such deep story. Trump's portrayal of himself as a victim—of the liberal media, of legal prosecutors, of nearly everyone—resonates with his supporters, building a connection with them as his brothers and sisters in victimhood.

In Kentucky, Hochschild also finds a version of a deep story she heard in Louisiana: crowds of white working-class people are patiently standing in line for the American Dream when suddenly minority groups push forward past them, waved ahead by Democrats. Enter a figure like Trump, who wins support for his willingness to target Democrats for their abuse of a rightful system. As one of Hochschild's subjects from Pike County concedes, Trump "has obvious flaws, but you forgive them because he's a *good* bully, strong enough to push around the *bad* bully," meaning the theft-enablers. "He's protecting you; he's *your* bully." The people Hochschild interviews often express resentment at being called racist "deplorables," as Hillary Clinton infamously said in 2016, and they bristle at the Democrats' "war on coal."

In calling this a deep story, Hochschild often suggests that ire for Democrats is irrational, an emotional narrative blind to the truth. Her subtext is that Appalachians' vote against Democrats is a vote against their interests, the policies that would improve their lives. "Joe Biden spoke of the rich 'paying their fair share' and passed legislation to try to regulate monopolies, protect labor unions, and increase taxes on the 1 percent," she reminds us, while "Republicans . . . have stronger faith . . . in capitalism without government help or regulation. . . . In the states they control, unregulated capitalism has given them a rougher ride." But nowhere does Hochschild indicate that Democrats bear any responsibility for the economic forces that *have* victimized Appalachians—including the "offshoring, automation, and union decline" she otherwise vividly describes.

The book focuses instead on white nationalist organizers—most notably Matthew Heimbach, former leader of the Traditionalist Worker Party, a neo-Nazi group he created in 2015 that would wind up at the center of Charlottesville's deadly Unite the Right rally in 2017. Hochschild's arrival in Pike County coincides with Heimbach's plans to recruit white-nationalists-to-be in the heart of Trump Country, and the fallout of his efforts carry the book's narrative along.

Like Trump, Heimbach leveraged the rhetoric of victimhood and stolen pride in his recruitment campaign. Unlike Trump, Heimbach failed spectacularly at his messaging. He lacked coherence, charisma, connections, and, most of all, power. His rally was poorly attended and beset with infighting, leaving Heimbach snubbed by the people he aimed to recruit by appealing to their whiteness. Hochschild dresses up Heimbach's failure as the casualty of two conflicting goals: the soft-pedaling of extremism, including racial separatism, for the sake of recruitment, and the building of solidarity among well-committed members of the far right.

On the ground, this looked like a parade of several hundred Nazi cosplayers, eager to flex their made-up tribalism among themselves as much as for their audience in the otherwise peaceful town of Pikeville, the county seat. Hochschild notes how cultural shame may have informed local reactions to the demonstration. She reveals, for example, a great sensitivity among the people she interviews toward common Appalachian stereotypes—as backward, uneducated, racist—and the ways they ricochet back onto the region in media coverage. Locals are embarrassed to be associated with Heimbach's demonstration, and before the march they are already dreading a spectacle that is sure to attract negative attention.

Does it matter to these same people that Trump's political ascendancy is a spectacle cut from a remarkably similar cloth, or that the goal of Heimbach's movement is to accelerate a complementary set of goals? Hochschild is much vaguer here, though she warns that "were fascism to enter the mainstream of American life... it would not appear in Nazi-like, swastika-brandishing uniform" or "through the fringe, or not only that way" but "through the ballot box." But we learn that Trump supporters in Pikeville, just like many of his supporters across the country, tend to disassociate themselves from the culture wars waged in their names. In *Stolen Pride*, we see them checking on their more vulnerable Black and Muslim neighbors, some even standing armed guard once the alt-right arrives, while remaining unreflective, in other contexts, about the implied danger of their politics.

As I explored whether Heimbach might be a victim of the pride paradox I felt an enormous sense of fatigue. Having lived through the aftermath of the Unite the Right rally, I reached the limits of my own emotional management. This backdrop also became distracting in a structural sense, with each chapter commencing with some variation of "Did you hear about the march?" It felt like Hochschild was missing part of the story about places like Pikeville—like these intermissions about pitiful white nationalists and Heimbach's failed marriage had taken the place of more vital and less heard perspectives. The book's lack of convincing justification for positioning Heimbach as a key informant raises more questions than it answers.

To be fair, Hochschild's openness to give anyone a hearing is balanced by the intentional selection of people of color, immigrants, prisoners, and others typically underrepresented in regional analysis. Nearly everyone Hochschild meets is a survivor of some form of disaster, whether the collapse of industry or the addiction crisis. Their stories are stories of loss. But the peculiarities of Appalachia and its demographic decline mean that the story of a place or people can't be told only through faces in the crowd. Appalachians, as a people, are also defined by our absences—the disowned youths and economic migrants.

When I was writing about Appalachia during the 2016 election, I was struck by how many people subscribed to the myth, which Hochschild might call a deep story, that a Trump victory would either force or tempt their children to return to the region. They seemed not to care whether the trigger was a total economic collapse or a bounty of riches. These voters in Appalachia were confident in stating the children of Appalachia would be returned. They weren't, of course.

This mythmaking, and how its unrealized hopes may have shaken the confidence of Appalachian Trump voters, would have made interesting material for *Stolen Pride*. Statistics are good at quantifying this loss—Pike County, for example, saw a 9.8 percent population decline between 2010 and 2020—but they fail to capture how this decline plays out generationally. How can political messaging better reach people who both mourn for their children and subscribe to politics that would annihilate their futures? What do these children think, feel, and experience in their lives outside of the region? These questions, and not the soap opera of white nationalist lives, would have made much more fertile ground.

BARBER, with Wilson-Hartgrove, is more interested in the story of these children. More rousing and polemical than *Stolen Pride*,

White Poverty examines poor white people writ large, although many happen to be from places like Pikeville. One example is a young white woman from Eastern Kentucky named Lakin, who watches her family grapple with the shame of unemployment. That shame became projected onto her when she came out, and she was disowned by her family and forced to live in her car. In Lakin's words, Barber hears that white poverty is "a curse that people are too often damned to bear alone."

A prominent pastor and movement leader in North Carolina, Barber has served as the president of the state's chapter of the NAACP and led several cross-racial protest campaigns. "I sound the alarm about white poverty," he writes, "because I'm convinced that we can't expose the peculiar exceptionalism of America's poverty without seeing how it impacts the very people that our myths pretend to privilege." Indeed, poor white people outnumber any other group experiencing poverty in the United States, he notes. The book debunks four myths impeding a complete understanding of poverty: that pale skin is a shared interest, that only Black folks want change in America, that poverty is only a Black issue, and that we can't overcome racial division. Barber is frustrated—rightly so—that people who aren't poor still imagine poverty to be an anomaly rather than a pervasive feature of American capitalism.

Barber finds isolation one of poverty's most salient aspects. Much like Hochschild, he argues that cultural messages about hard work and individualism, often deployed by politicians, have encouraged poor white people to absorb structural failures as their own. In order to hide their shame, these poor people conceal the traumas of their lives. These concealed losses become a void filled easily by politicians and billionaires, Barber argues, with "lies that tell us Black people are on one side of America's story, white people on the other." Barber explains—more fully than Hochschild—how myths about Black poverty cross racial lines and how, for some white people, the reality of experiencing a social status closer to poor Black people than middle-class or well-to-do whites intensifies feelings of shame.

Suffused with his biblical imagination and on-the-ground stories, the book also reflects on Barber's leadership of North Carolina's Moral Mondays Movement and, later, the national Poor People's Campaign. A corrective to our ways of talking about poverty, *White Poverty* is also a call for bottom-up organizing and shared connections among all poor people in an era of democratic renewal emphasizing racial and economic justice.

For Barber, this kind of "moral fusion" movement is both a strategic necessity—essential to building the coalitions we need in order to exercise power—and a historical fact. *White Poverty* looks to the Reconstruction Era's cross-racial coalition building, particularly in the South, to give white people in the present a claim to a lineage of justice seekers and endow the movement with unfinished purpose. In alliances between newly freed Black people and whites who recognized their economic fates as linked, the momentum for political change grew to such intensity that its enemies resorted to violence—such as the 1898 Wilmington massacre, which saw Wilmington's fusionist government ousted by white supremacists—to preserve their order. Later, these coalitions were revived again in the civil rights movement, a kind of Second Reconstruction. Barber calls for the revival of fusion among poor people across the nation—a Third Reconstruction uniting people of diverse backgrounds together in struggle. The Poor People's Campaign launched its latest season of outreach this June.

Schaller and Waldman are far less sympathetic to the plight of poor white people. "Since the rise of Jacksonian Democracy nearly two centuries ago," they write, "rural Whites have enjoyed what we call 'essential minority' status because they have been able to extract concessions from state governments and especially the national government that no other group of citizens of their size possibly could." This outsized power stems in part from malapportionment of the Senate. Enshrined in the Constitution, this form of representation gives a state like Wyoming, the least populated state, the same right to political representation as California, the most populated. As a result, government money that might have been spent on say, urban hospitals, gets sent to subsidize rural postal routes or airports. Schaller and Waldman make a similar argument about the Electoral College and the reversal of power that would be assured by replacing it with the popular vote. At the same time, they note, rural white people "are the *only* significant part of either party's coalition that has no coherent set of demands, for all the power they hold."

This sense of entitlement, the authors believe, has prompted increasingly large segments of the rural white population to react to social change with "belligerent contempt," seeking opportunities to air their rage and resentment at those who threaten their special status in American life. Schaller and Waldman argue that "rural White Americans assert a deep reverence for the Constitution and America's democratic principles" while at the same time harboring "anti-democratic attitudes" and a propensity "to use violence to carry out their political agenda"—what they call the "patriotic paradox." By way of comparison, the book points to the realities experienced by rural Black, Latino, and Native peoples, but it also refuses to define what "rural" actually is. Instead, the book extrapolates on research performed by academics in a variety of fields, some of whom have criticized *White Rural Rage* for over stating the prominence of extremist views among white rural Americans.

Although starkly different in tone, *White Poverty* and *White Rural Rage* both acknowledge that white people who want change, rural or poor or both, might simply not know how to organize. As Schaller and Waldman note, rural whites lack a model like the NAACP "with which to understand how politics is done and how it might affect their lives. There is no prominent National Association for the Advancement of Rural People lobbying and filing lawsuits on their behalf." In other parts of the country, white people might look toward unions (and therefore acknowledge the diversity among organizers of the actual working class) or white-specified ally spaces like the Showing Up for Racial Justice movement. Schaller and Waldman find the most potential for shake-up in demographic trends that suggest "steadily increasing diversity" in rural spaces, but they defer on suggesting an ideal approach. "We won't presume to tell rural Americans exactly what policies they should be asking for," they write. "That's something any movement has to decide on its own."

AS FOR outside observers, will *Stolen Pride* help in this political moment? I hope it does. Like Barber's, Hochschild's emphasis on unrecognized grief is a necessary corrective.

But Hochschild is more an explainer than a strategist. We can aim for "relief from the uneven burdens of the pride paradox," she counsels, "by revising the American Dream and by equalizing access to it." The closest she comes to plotting a concrete path forward is to stress "calm deliberation" and emotional understanding across partisan divides. "How does one person understand how another person got to feel the way he or she did?" she asks, looking to individuals unburdened by shame who can cross "the empathy bridge" within their communities.

This vision can sound like an out-of-touch sociologist's fantasy. There are limits to reducing politics to a matter of enlightened empathy and emotional intelligence, especially when unmoored from clear political demands and the kind of organizing and power building that Barber calls for. (As Hochschild admits, "To empathize is not to agree, or seek common ground"—though she hopes "these can more easily follow.") *Stolen Pride*'s key example of a "bridge-crosser" is a university chaplain who reacts to the news of the impending white nationalist march with calls for dialogue between the marchers and the community. To no one's surprise, Heimbach declines the invitation—as does the university chancellor, who staunchly opposes inviting the marchers on campus.

But the concept of community mediators isn't a bad idea in itself; as all organizers know, good mediation plays a pivotal role in holding coalitions together. Appalachia could use as many actual mediators as it can get—or really anyone trained to help address the staggering mental health crisis devastating the region. Appalachians have 50 percent fewer mental health care providers than the national average with a 17 percent higher risk of suicide. Our political discourse has tended to subsume these realities under the umbrella of "despair," but greater access to health care should be a standard talking point for anyone attempting to discuss the region's future.

The stories in *Stolen Pride* are not particularly deep if you've been close to the poverty line. After years of strategic abandonment by Democrats, a political figure that makes poor people feel seen and powerful takes a significant advantage. At a certain point, to what extent these individuals believe Trump will advance policies that materially improve their lives becomes literal white noise. The appeal is not the promises, but the attention and validation. Yet this moment offers an opportunity for pundits to learn from past mistakes and set aside some bafflement. As Schaller and Waldman argue, there is indeed an elevation of whiteness at work in the modern fixation on Appalachia, both regionally and nationally.

The larger question is what Democrats will offer poor white Americans. Will their nominee acknowledge, as Barber demands, that the horizon of our current political imagination fails to capture the realities of millions of lives lived on the precipice? What space will Democrats grant for the overdue public reckoning with the enormous sense of shame and grief carried by poor people across the nation? Weaponizing this shame has long been a bipartisan project with bipartisan benefits.

Stepping out from behind that truth might win the Democrats some advantages, as will concrete strategies to make housing more affordable, increase real wages, and expand access to health care that isn't contingent on one's ability to pay for it. The absolute worst they can do is retreat to moderate platitudes about achieving the American Dream.

CONTRIBUTORS

Tabatha Abu El-Haj is Professor of Law at Drexel University's Kline School of Law.

Danielle Allen is James Bryant Conant University Professor at Harvard and Director of the Allen Lab for Democracy Renovation at Harvard Kennedy School's Ash Center for Democratic Governance and Innovation. Her latest book is *Justice by Means of Democracy.*

Deepak Bhargava is President of the JPB Foundation and coauthor, with Stephanie Luce, of *Practical Radicals: Seven Strategies to Change the World.*

Elizabeth Catte is a writer and public historian based in the Shenandoah Valley, Virginia. She is the author of *Pure America: Eugenics and the Making of Modern Virginia* and *What You Are Getting Wrong about Appalachia.*

Kevin P. Donovan is Senior Lecturer at the Centre of African Studies, University of Edinburgh and author of *Money, Value, and the State: Sovereignty and Citizenship in East Africa.*

Lee Drutman is Senior Fellow in the Political Reform program at the New America Foundation. His books include *Breaking the Two-Party Doom Loop: The Case for Multiparty Democracy in America.*

James Goodwin is Policy Director at the Center for Progressive Reform.

Arianna Jiménez is Senior Vice President of Democracy, Gender, and Racial Justice at the JPB Foundation.

Josh Lerner is Co-Executive Director at People Powered.

Cerin Lindgrensavage is Counsel at Protect Democracy.

Bob Master was a founding co-chair of the New York State Working Families Party and worked for thirty-six years for the Communications Workers of America.

Maurice Mitchell is National Director of the Working Families Party.

Joel Rogers is Noam Chomsky Professor of Law, Public Affairs, and Sociology at the University of Wisconsin-Madison. He cofounded the New Party in 1990. His many books include *The Hidden Election*.

Sam Rosenfeld is Associate Professor of Political Science at Colgate University. His latest book, coauthored with Daniel Schlozman, is *The Hollow Parties: The Many Pasts and Disordered Present of American Party Politics*.

Daniel Schlozman is Associate Professor of Political Science at Johns Hopkins University. His latest book, coauthored with Sam Rosenfeld, is *The Hollow Parties: The Many Pasts and Disordered Present of American Party Politics*.

Doran Schrantz is Senior Strategist at Community Building Strategies.

Ian Shapiro is Sterling Professor of Political Science and Global Affairs at Yale. His books include *Responsible Parties: Saving Democracy from Itself*, coauthored with Frances Rosenbluth.

Honora Spicer is a PhD candidate in History at Harvard.

Sunaura Taylor is Assistant Professor in the Department of Environmental Science, Policy, & Management at the University of California, Berkeley. Her latest book is *Disabled Ecologies: Lessons from a Wounded Desert*.

Grant Tudor is Policy Advocate at Protect Democracy.

Rebecca Tuhus-Dubrow is is working on a book about the future of nuclear energy for Algonquin Books. Her writing has also appeared in the *New York Review of Books* and *The Guardian*.

David Austin Walsh is a postdoctoral associate at Yale and author of *Taking America Back: The Conservative Movement and the Far Right*.